FIRST EDITION

AN APOLOGY FOR IDLERS
AND OTHER ESSAYS

Robert Louis Stevenson

Edited by Matthew Kaiser

Bassim Hamadeh, CEO and Publisher
Kassie Graves, Director of Acquisitions and Sales
Jamie Giganti, Senior Managing Editor
Miguel Macias, Senior Graphic Designer
John Remington, Senior Field Acquisitions Editor
Gem Rabanera, Project Editor
Stephanie Kohl, Licensing Associate
Alia Bales, Associate Production Editor
Joyce Lue, Interior Designer

Trademark Notice: Product or corporate names may be trademarks or registered trademarks, and are used only for identification and explanation without intent to infringe.

ISBN: 978-1-5165-2164-7 (pbk) / 978-1-5165-5718-9 (br)

AN APOLOGY FOR IDLERS
AND OTHER ESSAYS

CONTENTS

INTRODUCTION

Idleness and the Essay: From Montaigne to Stevenson

> The soul that has no fixed goal loses itself; for as they say, to be everywhere is to be nowhere. —Michel de Montaigne[1]

An essay extolling the virtues of idleness is a contradiction in terms. One could even call it an "anti-essay." Consider the generic origins of the essay, or the etymology of the word. When Michel de Montaigne invented the essay in 1572, he did so with the express purpose of combatting the toxiferous effects of idleness. For "idleness," Montaigne lamented, "gives birth to . . . chimeras and fantastic monsters, one after another, without order or purpose."[2] "[I]n order to contemplate their ineptitude and strangeness at my pleasure," he announced, "I have begun to put them in writing, hoping in time to make my mind ashamed of itself." Montaigne christened his invention—his baggy amalgamation of personal and philosophical musings—the *essai*, which means "trial," "struggle," or "attempt" in French. Montaigne's essays are therapeutic devices, technologies of self-discipline. They are his attempts to overcome the depression into which he sank following the death of his friend Étienne de La Boétie. Psychological struggle and earnest self-cultivation are embedded, then, in the fabric of the modern essay, which was, from the start, a discursive exercise in purging the mind of lethargy.

1. Michel de Montaigne, "Of idleness," in *The Complete Works: Essays, Travel Journal, Letters*, trans. Donald M. Frame (New York and London: Everyman's Library, 2003), 24.
2. Ibid., 25.

In the late sixteenth and early seventeenth centuries, it was commonly believed that idlers—those who had stopped struggling or attempting—were more susceptible to melancholy than their counterparts, along with insomniacs, loners, gamblers, and people with overactive imaginations. Writing in 1638, Robert Burton observed that an "idle person . . . knows not when he is well, what he would have, or whither he would go," for "he is tired out with everything, displeased with all, weary of his life."[3] "[H]e wanders," Burton added, "and lives besides himself." In his *Essays* (1580–95), melancholic Montaigne set out in search of his wandering mind. To live not *beside* himself, or in spite of himself, but in the tumultuous midst of himself—this was his mission. He made his mind the locus of its scattered impressions, the center around which they swirled, rather than the passive landscape on which they rained destruction. Humanist philosopher that he was, Montaigne found himself—or rather, found a foothold in himself—not in theological systems or in totalizing theories of life, for which he had little patience. He found his foothold in the "back shop" (*arrière-boutique*) of his mind, as he called it.[4] From his "back shop," he fashioned discourse from disorder, took himself in hand: "Thus, reader, I am myself the matter of my book."[5] In a quiet tower in his chateau, halfway between Bergerac and Libourne, surrounded by the undulant fields of Dordogne, the death of his friend still gnawing at his heart, Montaigne invented the modern essay. A trained lawyer, counselor in the high court, and mayor, Montaigne did what he did best. He put his melancholy on trial. In finding a cure for idleness, in surveying his wandering thoughts, Montaigne took his place among the literary

---

3. Robert Burton, *The Anatomy of Melancholy, What It Is, with All the Kinds, Causes, Symptoms, Prognostics, and Several Cures of It* (Birmingham, AL: The Classics of Medicine Library, 1986), 160.
4. Montaigne, 214.
5. Ibid., 2.

inventors of modern subjectivity: Machiavelli and Shakespeare, Cervantes, Castiglione and Villon.

* * * * * *

Three hundred years later, Robert Louis Stevenson, a twenty-six-year-old law school graduate, pens "An Apology for Idlers" (1877). His law notebooks are covered in doodles. He abandons law after passing the bar. Stevenson's defense of idleness appears in the July issue of *The Cornhill Magazine*. It is not his first published essay, nor his first time working with prestigious *Cornhill*. The experience of writing this particular piece, however, releases, then clarifies, something in his mind—call it the wellspring of his worldview. Other essays follow in a similar vein. At first blush, Stevenson seems an unlikely candidate for greatness. His parents still pay his bills. He falls in love too easily. He corresponds on a regular basis with his childhood nurse. Five foot ten, weighing less than 125 pounds, he looks insubstantial. Yet six years later Stevenson achieves greatness with *Treasure Island* (1883), followed in 1886 by *Kidnapped* and *Strange Case of Dr. Jekyll and Mr. Hyde*. The spark that ignited that greatness is "An Apology for Idlers": his provocative "anti-essay," his attempt *not* to attempt, his struggle against struggling. Stevenson's intricate and elegant essays—fifteen of which are collected in this volume—celebrate idleness and its allied arts: play, immaturity, truancy, insomnia, recklessness, invalidism, mischief-making, permissiveness, languor, and wanderlust. For before he earned a reputation as a masterful short-story writer and novelist, Stevenson was known, by the few readers who knew him, as a skilled essayist and travel writer. These are the seeds that he planted in his vagabond garden: the window boxes of his readers. We wake to blossoms. In the essays that follow—all but two of which were published between 1874 and 1888 (his juvenile sketches "Nuits Blanches" and "Nurses" were published posthumously in 1896)—Stevenson proclaims the idler and his crew to be model citizens, philosophers of love, founts of unacknowledged wisdom. He urges readers to follow the trill of Pan's pipes to the precipice of consciousness. He invites us to rethink modern subjectivity: to conceive of ourselves as points of departure rather than as towers of surveillance.

What are we to make of Stevenson's metageneric acts of devil's advocacy, his upstart essays? While most contemporary reviewers were charmed, one grumbled that young Stevenson thumbs his nose at readers, struts about with his tongue in his cheek. How seriously are we to take Stevenson's idle pronouncements? Do they mask the thing he claims to despise the most: ambition? While Stevenson certainly hoped to make a living from writing, ambition, the scramble for coin and place, was never his forte. A failed lawyer, a failed engineer, a chronic wanderer, a repeat visitor to alpine sanitaria, an opium enthusiast, Stevenson was nearly destroyed—physically and emotionally—by the Victorian cult of ambition, by the masculine imperative that he make his family proud. This does not mean, therefore, that he took his craft lightly. He loses himself in writing, tumbles down the rabbit hole—as a child loses herself in a favorite toy. Imagination is Stevenson's refuge from ambition, a means of letting go of his doubt-plagued self. At the end of his life, in the South Pacific, he lets go his name and adopts a Samoan moniker, Tusitala ("Storyteller"), defining himself by what he loves doing rather than by genealogy or by his critically acclaimed initials.

The idler does not seek wisdom and enlightenment in self-discipline, education, or trials of strength. Nor does he keep his "eye on the medal." Wisdom finds him by accident. It gathers at the side of the road, or on a riverbank, in the feral afternoons of troubadours and layabouts and truant schoolboys, whose singsong voices and bawdy nonchalance Montaigne heard, too, in his tower, in snatches, on sultry winds from country lanes. Where Montaigne resisted, Stevenson succumbs. He descends the spiral stair, follows the meandering strain. Stevenson chooses as his guide in life the maligned idler, who goes nowhere but is "a great deal in the open air." Only idlers escape the epistemological pitfalls of the "dogmatists." Only idlers dodge the bullets of busyness. Only idlers understand "the Art of Living":

> Extreme *busyness*, whether at school or college, kirk or market, is a symptom of deficient vitality; and a faculty for idleness implies a catholic appetite and a strong sense of personal identity. There is a sort of dead-alive, hackneyed people about, who are scarcely conscious of living except in the exercise of some conventional occupation. Bring these fellows into the country, or set them aboard ship, and you will see how they pine for their desk or their study. They have no curiosity; they cannot give themselves over to random provocations; they do not take pleasure in the exercise of their faculties for its own sake; and unless Necessity lays about them with a stick, they will even stand still. It is no good speaking to such folk: they *cannot* be idle, their nature is not generous enough; and they pass those hours in a sort of coma, which are not dedicated to furious moiling in the gold-mill.

Stevenson rattles the essay's ideological cage. He shakes the industrious foundations of subjectivity. He does for the essay what Wordsworth did for the ballad. Stevenson pokes fun at professionalism and money-grubbing and respectability and self-importance. He mocks the work ethic of his parents and their friends. He bemoans the weaponization of our intellects by capitalist competition. The marketplace, he fears, has transformed Montaigne's lonely little "back shop" into an arsenal, or sweatshop, or both, where thoughts are optimized, retooled, made instruments of control and focus. With "An Apology for Idlers," Stevenson "tries to relieve us," Stephen Arata explains, "of the burden of paying attention, or more precisely, he encourages us to reimagine attention as a more dispersed and decentered phenomenon, one capable of inducing that ecstatic stupor he so valued."[6] Stevenson's essays promote a different—less goal-oriented, more nomadic—mode of life and style of seeing. Vagabondage begins when we cease *working* on ourselves, lose ourselves along the byways, in the speckled groves, of life. Don't take yourself so seriously, he whispers in our ear. Rather than recall our wandering thoughts, he implores us to scatter ourselves to the four winds. Whitman might contain multitudes, but Stevenson is a one-man diaspora.

For all their loveliness, their flashes of radicalism, or their intricate network of literary and biblical reference, Stevenson's essays tend to be modest in scope and scale. Some are even trifling. They concern themselves with minor subjects: the play of children, or a sleepless night, or the pleasure of ducking behind a wall on a windy day. He is drawn to phenomena generally considered beneath essayistic notice: to the blind spots in our day and to the people we see out the corner of our eye, whom we blink away. Even his forays into irrationalism and relativism (What does it matter, we're all going to die!) are tempered with Scottish common sense and an undying politeness. He apologizes for having troubled us. Politically, Stevenson tiptoes toward naughtiness but avoids anything that smacks of revolution. He is a Tory in his distrust of future-directed schemes and in his affection for the past, a socialist in his disgust at greed and in his rejection of hierarchy, a

6. Stephen Arata, "Stevenson, Morris, and the Value of Idleness," in *Robert Louis Stevenson: Writer of Boundaries*, eds. Richard Ambrosini and Richard Dury (Madison: University of Wisconsin Press, 2006), 11.

hipster *avant la lettre* in his world-weary irony. A bit disingenuously, he presents himself as inconsequential, a nobody, a friend for an hour, though it is *his* consciousness we inhabit. The more famous he gets, the more self-deprecating his narrative voice becomes. By 1888, he has embraced the persona of well-meaning bumbler or wallflower, a man more at ease with the village beggar than with his businessman neighbor. Stevenson is forever out of place. He delights in emasculating himself. He wears boyish awkwardness as a badge of honor. Even as he limns a blustery seascape, he complains about having an earache. No wonder some of his male readers—his father, for instance—cringe. Stevenson doesn't care. Idleness is self-abasement. By refusing to tower over others, to soar rhetorically and conceptually like a Carlyle or an Arnold, Stevenson turns essay-writing on its head. Nothing—he insists—is more depressing than purpose, or self-preservation, or beating a gaggle of brains into submission. Nothing poisons the soul like a fighting spirit.

Stevenson has no interest in playing hero or leading man, and certainly not Victorian sage. Nor does he claim to be a pioneer in his beloved art of idleness. Even in idling, he plays second fiddle. He is not the first essayist, he reminds us, to sing its praises. His idle idol, the indefatigable Samuel Johnson, beat him to the punch by one hundred and twenty years. Though Stevenson never quotes *The Idler* (1758–60) directly, Johnson's name appears frequently in his essays (more often than Montaigne's, or Scott's, or Burns's, for that matter). Stevenson doffs his hat every time. He drops it once, the klutz, misquoting Boswell's *The Life of Dr. Johnson* (1791) in his epigraph to "An Apology for Idlers." Written on the eve of the Industrial Revolution, Johnson's *The Idler* anticipates Stevenson's essays in obvious ways: in its charmingly wry tone, its revaluation of idleness as an intellectual virtue, and its equation of idling with life. "The Idler, though sluggish," Johnson declares in his first number, "is yet alive."[7] In these and other ways, Stevenson follows in the jittery footsteps of the caffeinated lexicographer. But Johnsonian idleness differs, in key respects, from its Stevensonian second cousin. Johnson finds manly purpose in idleness. Idleness is the telos of industry, life's reward. It is another kind of work, more refined, more rarefied, but work nonetheless. Rather than scatter our psyche, Johnsonian idleness renders us coherent. In an age of increased leisure, idleness binds our subjectivity. Over the course of ninety-one essays, Johnson dismantles the wall between London's coffeehouses and Montaigne's "back shop." He reconciles the idler and the essay. He makes the essay format safe for the idler, makes idleness safe for the essay-writer. Under Johnson's pacifying quill, idleness becomes ambitious, aspirational, heroic:

> Every man is, or hopes to be, an Idler. Even those who seem to differ most from us are hastening to increase our fraternity; as peace is the end of war, so to be idle is the ultimate purpose of the busy.[8]

Here Stevenson parts company with Johnson. He cannot bring himself to travel any path, no matter how charming his companion, that leads *somewhere*. Stevenson flees the broad boulevards of tomorrow, our means-to-an-end culture, a value system that subordinates the idle pleasures of the moment to the demands of the future. The telic—the purpose-driven—nature of Johnsonian idleness is antithetical to Stevenson's love of detours and meandering trails and peripateticism. Though he is not anti-intellectual, Stevenson is anti-educational in his outlook. Institutions of higher learning shackle and shrink our minds. His autobiographical essay "The Education of an Engineer" (1888) recalls with fondness the

---

7. Samuel Johnson, "No. 1. The Idler's Character: Saturday, April 15, 1758," in *The Works of Samuel Johnson*, Vol. 7 (London: Thomas Tegg, 1824), 4.
8. Ibid., 2.

truant spirit that ends his career as an engineer before it begins. Sent to Wick in northern Scotland to assist in the construction of a seawall, apprentice Stevenson loses himself instead in vagabond activities. Rather than advance briskly through life, accumulating knowledge, learning to hold back the sea, like some Canute-in-training, Stevenson wanders the countryside near Wick, writes midnight poetry, dons a diving apparatus and treads the floor of the North Sea in slow motion—a submarine idler. How different he is from his plotting, driven colleagues! The ambitious engineer embodies, in Stevenson's eyes, the hubristic spirit of the Victorian Age. The engineers who built the Tower of Babel were ambitious too, he reminds us. In the end, our schemes collapse. Towers crumble. Death builds his house at the end of every street. Like those alienated babblers, those failed engineers whom God scattered to the four corners of the earth, nomadic Stevenson turns his attention to cultivating his voice.

Stevenson's essays seduce, rather than educate. Like Boccaccio, Villon, Byron, Baudelaire, and Kerouac, Stevenson is one of literature's great seducers. He leads readers astray. The Latin verb *educere* means "to lead forth" or "to draw out." As far as Latin verbs go, it is not Stevenson's favorite. His sympathies lie with the less respectable *seducere*, which means "to draw aside" or "to lead or carry away." Stevenson has no interest in acting as our teacher. His truant essays waylay us from the side, urge us to unlearn our lessons, to wander aimlessly at his side, or to strike out on our own. To borrow a phrase from Gabriel García Márquez, Stevenson gives us "an eternal ticket on a train that never stopped travelling."[9] His essays are all detours and distractions, temptations and departures: the tickle of sun-drenched grass, the lingering glance of a stranger, a ruined castle on the Scottish coast. The idler turns his back on his future. What does the future

9. Gabriel García Márquez, *One Hundred Years of Solitude*, trans. Gregory Rabassa (New York: Everyman's Library, 1998), 402.

hold for us, Stevenson asks, but "a rough, war-faring existence"? Wisdom is a sideward movement; it is off road.

If Stevenson shrinks from what lies ahead, if he clings a little too eagerly to the romance of youth, it is because, poor fellow, he was dying. Stevensonian idleness is the art of dodging death. In *New Arabian Nights* (1882), his first book of short stories, he compares himself to Scheherazade, who weaves her seductive webs in order that she might escape the executioner's blade and live another day. Diagnosed with "delicate" (pretubercular) lungs at age twenty-three and with full-blown tuberculosis at twenty-nine, Stevenson was prone to viral infections, impaired vision, fatigue, depression, migraines, and, for the last fifteen years of his life, pulmonary hemorrhaging. He barely escapes death in San Francisco in 1880, drowning in fever and blood, the ocean fog inflaming his lungs. Another sideward movement, this time by ferry to Oakland, saves his life. Stevenson lived in the shadow of death, like those "South American citizens" who "live upon the side of fiery mountains." "[W]hat, pathologically looked at, is the human body with all its organs," he asks, "but a mere bagful of petards?" With each shallow breath or blood-flecked cough, Stevenson hears the ticking bomb in his chest. We know now that his doctors got it wrong. His body harbored an altogether different threat. Given the fact that "advanced bacillus tests" on his sputum came back negative, medical historians, Clare Harman writes, now believe that Stevenson "may have suffered from haemorrhagic telangiectasia, or Osler-Rendu-Weber Syndrome."[10] This would explain his bouts of pulmonary hemorrhaging and his death at age forty-four from massive cerebral hemorrhage. Is it any wonder, then, that Stevenson travels backward or sideways or downward in his writings, zigging and zagging, losing himself

10. Claire Harman, *Myself and the Other Fellow: A Life of Robert Louis Stevenson* (New York: HarperCollins, 2005), 332.

in the South Seas or the Highlands, or chasing the setting sun west—that he goes every which way but forward?

* * * * * *

The modern essay began life as a contemplation of death. Death haunts it still. Montaigne found the strength to mourn his friend Étienne de La Boétie in essay-writing, in taming his idle, melancholic thoughts. His essays gave him purpose. They taught him to move forward. Three centuries later, Robert Louis Stevenson quits the funeral procession that is the modern essay. He invites us to join him at the side of the road. Why the hurry? Nothing good lies down *that* road, he insists. That way lies "offices and the witness-box": trials and struggles and attempts. It is a mournful business. Let's stop here for the night, where we will have "no other tent but the sky, and no other bed than my mother earth."[11]

11. Robert Louis Stevenson, *Travels with a Donkey in the Cevennes*, in *The Works of Robert Louis Stevenson*, Vol. 1, ed. Edmund Gosse (London: Cassell, 1906), 248.

A NOTE ON THE TEXT

With a few minor exceptions, the texts in this volume follow the Pentland Edition of *The Works of Robert Louis Stevenson* (1906–7), which was edited by Stevenson's friend and fellow writer Edmund Gosse and published in twenty volumes in London by Cassell (in association with Chatto & Windus, William Heinemann, and Longmans Green & Company). Below, however, is the publication history of the fifteen essays collected in this volume:

"An Apology for Idlers." *Cornhill Magazine* 36 (July 1877). Later included in Stevenson's first book of essays, *Virginibus Puerisque and Other Papers* (London: Kegan Paul, 1881).

"Pan's Pipes." *London* (May 1878). Included in *Virginibus Puerisque* (1881).

"Æs Triplex." *Cornhill Magazine* 37 (April 1878). Included in *Virginibus Puerisque* (1881).

"The Education of an Engineer" [originally titled "The Education of an Engineer: More Random Memories"]. *Scribner's Magazine* 4 (November 1888). Later included in Stevenson's *Across the Plains with Other Memories and Essays* (London: Chatto & Windus, 1892).

"François Villon, Student, Poet, Housebreaker." *Cornhill Magazine* 36 (August 1877). Later included in Stevenson's *Familiar Studies of Men and Books* (London: Chatto & Windus, 1882).

"Crabbed Age and Youth." *Cornhill Magazine* 37 (March 1878). Included in *Virginibus Puerisque* (1881).

"A Letter to a Young Gentleman who Proposes to Embrace the Career of Art." *Scribner's Magazine* 4 (September 1888). Included in *Across the Plains* (1892).

"Beggars." *Scribner's Magazine* 3 (March 1888). Included in *Across the Plains* (1892).

"Ordered South." *Macmillan's Magazine* 30 (May 1874). Included in *Virginibus Puerisque* (1881).

"Child's Play." *Cornhill Magazine* 38 (September 1878). Included in *Virginibus Puerisque* (1881).

"The Stimulation of the Alps." *Pall Mall Gazette* (March 5, 1881).

"Nurses." Written c.1871. Published posthumously in the Edinburgh Edition of *The Works of Robert Louis Stevenson*, Vol. 21: *Juvenilia and Other Papers*, ed. Sidney Colvin (London: Charles Baxter and Sidney Colvin, 1896).

"San Francisco" [originally titled "A Modern Cosmopolis"]. *The Magazine of Art* 6 (May 1883). Included in the Edinburgh Edition of *The Works of Robert Louis Stevenson*, Vol. 3: *Travels and Excursions*, ed. Sidney Colvin (London: Charles Baxter and Sidney Colvin, 1895).

"Nuits Blanches." Written c.1871. Published posthumously in the Edinburgh Edition of *The Works of Robert Louis Stevenson*, Vol. 21: *Juvenilia and Other Papers*, ed. Sidney Colvin (London: Charles Baxter and Sidney Colvin, 1896).

"On the Enjoyment of Unpleasant Places." *The Portfolio* 5 (November 1874).

THE ESSAYS

AN APOLOGY FOR IDLERS

BOSWELL: We grow weary when idle.
JOHNSON: That is, sir, because others being busy, we want company; but if we were idle, there would be no growing weary; we should all entertain one another.[1]

Just now, when everyone is bound, under pain of a decree in absence convicting them of *lèse*-respectability,[2] to enter on some lucrative profession, and labour therein with something not far short of enthusiasm, a cry from the opposite party who are content when they have enough, and like to look on and enjoy in the meanwhile, savours a little of bravado and gasconade.[3] And yet this should not be. Idleness so called, which does not consist in doing nothing, but in doing a great deal not recognized in the dogmatic formularies of the ruling class, has as good a right to

1. From *The Life of Dr. Johnson* (1791) by James Boswell (1740–1795), Scottish diarist and biographer. The conversation between Boswell and Samuel Johnson (1709–1784), English essayist, poet and lexicographer, occurred on October 26, 1769 at the Mitre Tavern in London. Stevenson misquotes Boswell. Johnson's response should read: "but if we are all idle, there would be no growing weary; we should all entertain one another."
2. A crime of high treason, *lèse-majesté* means to demean the majesty or dignity of the monarch. Those charged with Stevenson's fictitious crime of "*lèse*-respectability" insult middle-class values.
3. Boasting.

state its position as industry itself. It is admitted that the presence of people who refuse to enter in the great handicap race for sixpenny pieces, is at once an insult and a disenchantment for those who do. A fine fellow (as we see so many) takes his determination, votes for the sixpences, and, in the emphatic Americanism, "goes for" them. And while such an one is ploughing distressfully up the road, it is not hard to understand his resentment, when he perceives cool persons in the meadows by the wayside, lying with a handkerchief over their ears and a glass at their elbow. Alexander is touched in a very delicate place by the disregard of Diogenes.[4] Where was the glory of having taken Rome for these tumultuous barbarians, who poured into the Senate house, and found the Fathers sitting silent and unmoved by their success?[5] It is a sore thing to have laboured along and scaled the arduous hill-tops, and when all is done, find humanity indifferent to your achievement. Hence physicists condemn the unphysical; financiers have only a superficial toleration for those who know little of stocks; literary persons despise the unlettered; and people of all pursuits combine to disparage those who have none.

But though this is one difficulty of the subject, it is not the greatest. You could not be put in prison for speaking against industry, but you can be sent to Coventry[6] for speaking like a fool. The greatest difficulty with most subjects is to do them well; therefore, please to remember this is an apology. It is certain that much may be judiciously argued in favour of diligence; only there is

4. Plutarch (AD 46 – AD 120) describes the incident in his biography of Alexander the Great (356 BC – 323 BC). Alexander travelled to Corinth expressly to meet Diogenes of Sinope (c.412 BC – 323 BC). He found him lounging in the sun. When he asked Diogenes how he could be of service, the philosopher responded: "Stand a little out of my sun." An amused Alexander declared: "If I were not Alexander, I would be Diogenes!"
5. The Senones, a Gallic people, invaded Rome in 390 BC. When they entered the palaces of the patricians, they were greeted with haughty contempt.
6. "To send someone to Coventry" means to ostracize or shun that person. When Royalist troops were captured in Birmingham during the English Civil War (1642–51), they were sent to the city of Coventry, then a Parliamentarian stronghold, where they received a chilly reception.

something to be said against it, and that is what, on the present occasion, I have to say. To state one argument is not necessarily to be deaf to all others, and that a man has written a book of travels in Montenegro, is no reason why he should never have been to Richmond.

It is surely beyond a doubt that people should be a good deal idle in youth. For though here and there a Lord Macaulay[7] may escape from school honours with all his wits about him, most boys pay so dear for their medals that they never afterwards have a shot in their locker,[8] and begin the world bankrupt. And the same holds true during all the time a lad is educating himself, or suffering others to educate him. It must have been a very foolish old gentleman who addressed Johnson at Oxford in these words: "Young man, ply your book diligently now, and acquire a stock of knowledge; for when years come upon you, you will find that poring upon books will be but an irksome task."[9] The old gentleman seems to have been unaware that many other things besides reading grow irksome, and not a few become impossible, by the time a man has to use spectacles and cannot walk without a stick. Books are good enough in their own way, but they are a mighty bloodless substitute for life. It seems a pity to sit, like the Lady of Shalott,[10] peering into a mirror, with your back turned on all the bustle and glamour of reality. And if a man reads very hard, as the old anecdote reminds us, he will have little time for thought.

If you look back on your own education, I am sure it will not be the full, vivid, instructive hours of truantry that you regret; you

---

7. Thomas Babington Macaulay (1800–1859), English politician, historian and essayist. When he was a young man, Macaulay taught himself several European languages and earned multiple prizes at Cambridge University.
8. Have no money or opportunity left.
9. Johnson shared this memory with Boswell in 1763 at the Turk's Head coffee-house in London.
10. Alfred Tennyson's poem "The Lady of Shalott" (1833) is the story of a cursed woman who sits alone in a tower, weaving images of the world reflected in her mirror. Weary at last of reflections of reflections, she abandons her loom and her tower and enters the world, whereupon she dies.

would rather cancel some lackluster periods between sleep and waking in the class. For my own part, I have attended a good many lectures in my time. I still remember that the spinning of a top is a case of Kinetic Stability. I still remember that Emphyteusis[11] is not a disease, nor Stillicide[12] a crime. But though I would not willingly part with such scraps of science, I do not set the same store by them as by certain other odds and ends that I came by in the open street while I was playing truant. This is not the moment to dilate on that mighty place of education, which was the favourite school of Dickens and of Balzac,[13] and turns out yearly many inglorious masters in the Science of the Aspects of Life. Suffice it to say this: if a lad does not learn in the streets, it is because he has no faculty of learning. Nor is the truant always in the streets, for if he prefers, he may go out by the gardened suburbs into the country. He may pitch on some tuft of lilacs over a burn,[14] and smoke innumerable pipes to the tune of the water on the stones. A bird will sing in the thicket, and there he may fall into a vein of kindly thought, and see things in a new perspective. Why, if this be not education, what is? We may conceive Mr. Worldly Wiseman[15] accosting such an one, and the conversation that should thereupon ensue:—

"How now, young fellow, what dost thou here?"

"Truly, sir, I take mine ease."

"Is not this the hour of the class? and shouldst thou not be plying thy Book with diligence, to the end thou mayest obtain knowledge?"

---

11. In Roman law, *emphyteusis* refers to a contract to lease land in perpetuity on the condition that the lessee improve the property.
12. In Roman law, stillicide refers to the right to collect water dripping from a neighbor's roof onto one's property.
13. Charles Dickens (1812–1870) and French novelist Honoré de Balzac (1799–1850) were pioneers of literary realism.
14. A creek.
15. Mr. Worldly Wiseman is a character in *The Pilgrim's Progress* (1678), a Christian allegory, by Puritan preacher John Bunyan (1628–1688). A resident of the Town of Carnal Policy, and a mouthpiece for secular ethics, Mr. Worldly Wiseman waylays Christian on his journey to the Celestial City and tries to convince him that legality and civility are sufficient organizing principles for society.

"Nay, but thus also I follow after Learning, by your leave."

"Learning, quotha![16] After what fashion, I pray thee? Is it mathematics?"

"No, to be sure."

"Is it metaphysics?"

"Nor that."

"Is it some language?"

"Nay, it is no language."

"Is it a trade?"

"Nor a trade neither."

"Why, then, what is't?"

"Indeed, sir, as a time may soon come for me to go upon Pilgrimage, I am desirous to note what is commonly done by persons in my case, and where are the ugliest Sloughs[17] and Thickets on the Road; as also, what manner of Staff is of the best service. Moreover, I lie here, by this water, to learn by root-of-heart a lesson which my master teaches me to call Peace, or Contentment."

Hereupon Mr. Worldly Wiseman was much commoved with passion, and shaking his cane with a very threatful countenance, broke forth upon this wise: "Learning, quotha!" said he; "I would have all such rogues scourged by the Hangman!"

And so he would go on his way, ruffling out his cravat with a crackle of starch, like a turkey when it spreads its feathers.

Now this, of Mr. Wiseman's, is the common opinion. A fact is not called a fact, but a piece of gossip, if it does not fall into one of your scholastic categories. An inquiry must be in some acknowledged direction, with a name to go by; or else you are not inquiring at all, only lounging; and the workhouse[18] is too good for you. It is supposed that all knowledge is at the bottom

16. A sarcastic "indeed!" that typically follows a word or phrase one is quoting.
17. In *The Pilgrim's Progress*, Christian must navigate various spiritual obstacles on his path to God, including the Slough of Despond, a swamp of sin and guilt.
18. In nineteenth-century Britain, the workhouse was a public institution where the destitute and homeless were provided food and shelter in return for work.

of a well, or the far end of a telescope. Sainte-Beuve,[19] as he grew older, came to regard all experience as a single great book, in which to study for a few years ere we go hence; and it seemed all one to him whether you should read in Chapter XX, which is the differential calculus, or in Chapter XXXIX, which is hearing the band play in the gardens. As a matter of fact, an intelligent person, looking out of his eyes and hearkening in his ears, with a smile on his face all the time, will get more true education than many another in a life of heroic vigils. There is certainly some chill and arid knowledge to be found upon the summits of formal and laborious science; but it is all round about you, and for the trouble of looking, that you will acquire the warm and palpitating facts of life. While others are filling their memory with a lumber of words, one-half of which they will forget before the week be out, your truant may learn some really useful art: to play the fiddle, to know a good cigar, or to speak with ease and opportunity to all varieties of men. Many who have "plied their book diligently," and know all about some one branch or another of accepted lore, come out of the study with an ancient and owl-like demeanour, and prove dry, stockish,[20] and dyspeptic in all the better and brighter parts of life. Many make a large fortune, who remain under-bred and pathetically stupid to the last. And meantime there goes the idler, who began life along with them—by your leave, a different picture. He has had time to take care of his health and his spirits; he has been a great deal in the open air, which is the most salutary of all things for both body and mind; and if he has never read the great Book in very recondite places, he has dipped into it and skimmed it over to excellent purpose. Might not the student afford some Hebrew roots, and the business man some of his half-crowns, for a share of the idler's knowledge of life at large, and Art of Living? Nay, and the idler has another and more important quality than

19. Charles Augustin Sainte-Beuve (1804–1869), French literary critic.
20. Stupid.

these. I mean his wisdom. He who has much looked on at the childish satisfaction of other people in their hobbies, will regard his own with only a very ironical indulgence. He will not be heard among the dogmatists. He will have a great and cool allowance for all sorts of people and opinions. If he finds no out-of-the-way truths, he will identify himself with no very burning falsehood. His way takes him along a by-road, not much frequented, but very even and pleasant, which is called Commonplace Lane, and leads to the Belvedere[21] of Commonsense. Thence he shall command an agreeable, if no very noble prospect; and while others behold the East and West, the Devil and the Sunrise, he will be contentedly aware of a sort of morning hour upon all sublunary things, with an army of shadows running speedily and in many different directions into the great daylight of Eternity. The shadows and the generations, the shrill doctors and the plangent[22] wars, go by into ultimate silence and emptiness; but underneath all this, a man may see, out of the Belvedere windows, much green and peaceful landscape; many fire-lit parlours; good people laughing, drinking, and making love, as they did before the Flood or the French Revolution; and the old shepherd telling his tale under the hawthorn.

Extreme *busyness*, whether at school or college, kirk[23] or market, is a symptom of deficient vitality; and a faculty for idleness implies a catholic appetite and a strong sense of personal identity. There is a sort of dead-alive, hackneyed people about, who are scarcely conscious of living except in the exercise of some conventional occupation. Bring these fellows into the country, or set them aboard ship, and you will see how they pine for their desk or their study. They have no curiosity; they cannot give themselves over to random provocations; they do not take pleasure in the exercise of their faculties for its own sake; and unless Necessity

21. A building or structure that commands a beautiful or sweeping view.
22. Loud and plaintive.
23. Church.

lays about them with a stick, they will even stand still. It is no good speaking to such folk: they *cannot* be idle, their nature is not generous enough; and they pass those hours in a sort of coma, which are not dedicated to furious moiling in the gold-mill. When they do not require to go to the office, when they are not hungry and have no mind to drink, the whole breathing world is a blank to them. If they have to wait an hour or so for a train, they fall into a stupid trance with their eyes open. To see them, you would suppose there was nothing to look at and no one to speak with; you would imagine they were paralyzed or alienated; and yet very possibly they are hard workers in their own way, and have good eyesight for a flaw in a deed or a turn of the market. They have been to school and college, but all the time they had their eye on the medal; they have gone about in the world and mixed with clever people, but all the time they were thinking of their own affairs. As if a man's soul were not too small to begin with, they have dwarfed and narrowed theirs by a life of all work and no play; until here they are at forty, with a listless attention, a mind vacant of all material of amusement, and not one thought to rub against another, while they wait for the train. Before he was breeched,[24] he might have clambered on the boxes; when he was twenty, he would have stared at the girls; but now the pipe is smoked out, the snuff-box empty, and my gentleman sits bolt upright upon a bench, with lamentable eyes. This does not appeal to me as being Success in Life.

But it is not only the person himself who suffers from his busy habits, but his wife and children, his friends and relations, and down to the very people he sits with in a railway carriage or an omnibus. Perpetual devotion to what a man calls his business, is only to be sustained by perpetual neglect of many other things. And it is not by any means certain that a man's business is the

24. To be "breeched" means to be dressed for the first time in trousers or breeches. Prior to breeching, young boys wore dresses for purposes of toilet training.

most important thing he has to do. To an impartial estimate it will seem clear that many of the wisest, most virtuous, and most beneficent parts that are to be played upon the Theatre of Life are filled by gratuitous performers, and pass, among the world at large, as phases of idleness. For in that Theatre, not only the walking gentlemen, singing chambermaids, and diligent fiddlers in the orchestra, but those who look on and clap their hands from the benches, do really play a part and fulfil important offices towards the general result. You are no doubt very dependent on the care of your lawyer and stockbroker, of the guards and signalmen[25] who convey you rapidly from place to place, and the policemen who walk the streets for your protection; but is there not a thought of gratitude in your heart for certain other benefactors who set you smiling when they fall in your way, or season your dinner with good company? Colonel Newcome helped to lose his friend's money; Fred Bayham had an ugly trick of borrowing shirts; and yet they were better people to fall among than Mr. Barnes.[26] And though Falstaff[27] was neither sober nor very honest, I think I could name one or two long-faced Barabbases[28] whom the world could better have done without. Hazlitt mentions that he was more sensible of obligation to Northcote,[29] who had never done him anything he could call a service, than to his whole circle of ostentatious friends; for he thought a good companion emphatically the greatest benefactor. I know there are people in the world who cannot feel grateful unless the favour has been done

25. A railway signal-box operator.

26. Colonel Thomas Newcome and Frederick Bayham are characters in the novel *The Newcomes* (1855) by William Makepeace Thackeray (1811–1863). Barnes Newcome is the Colonel's snobbish and conniving nephew.

27. A fat, humorous and cowardly knight who appears in several of Shakespeare's plays.

28. Pontius Pilate, the Roman governor of Judea, grants the angry mob the power to free one of two men from prison: Jesus or Barabbas, a murderer. They choose Barabbas.

29. In *Conversations of James Northcote* (1830), English essayist William Hazlitt (1778–1830) recounts his impressions of the charismatic painter.

them at the cost of pain and difficulty. But this is a churlish disposition. A man may send you six sheets of letter-paper covered with the most entertaining gossip, or you may pass half an hour pleasantly, perhaps profitably, over an article of his; do you think the service would be greater, if he had made the manuscript in his heart's blood, like a compact with the devil? Do you really fancy you should be more beholden to your correspondent, if he had been damning you all the while for your importunity? Pleasures are more beneficial than duties because, like the quality of mercy, they are not strained, and they are twice blest. There must always be two to a kiss, and there may be a score in a jest; but wherever there is an element of sacrifice, the favour is conferred with pain, and, among generous people, received with confusion. There is no duty we so much underrate as the duty of being happy. By being happy, we sow anonymous benefits upon the world, which remain unknown even to ourselves, or when they are disclosed, surprise nobody so much as the benefactor. The other day, a ragged, barefoot boy ran down the street after a marble, with so jolly an air that he set everyone he passed into a good humour; one of these persons, who had been delivered from more than usually black thoughts, stopped the little fellow and gave him some money with this remark: "You see what sometimes comes of looking pleased." If he had looked pleased before, he had now to look both pleased and mystified. For my part, I justify this encouragement of smiling rather than tearful children; I do not wish to pay for tears anywhere but upon the stage; but I am prepared to deal largely in the opposite commodity. A happy man or woman is a better thing to find than a five-pound note. He or she is a radiating focus of good will; and their entrance into a room is as though another candle had been lighted. We need not care whether they could prove the forty-seventh proposition;[30] they do a better thing

30. The Pythagorean theorem, or forty-seventh proposition of Euclid, states that, in any right triangle, the sum of the squares of the two sides is equal to the square of the hypotenuse.

than that, they practically demonstrate the great Theorem of the Liveableness of Life. Consequently, if a person cannot be happy without remaining idle, idle he should remain. It is a revolutionary precept; but, thanks to hunger and the workhouse, one not easily to be abused, and, within practical limits, it is one of the most incontestable truths in the whole Body of Morality. Look at one of your industrious fellows for a moment, I beseech you. He sows hurry and reaps indigestion; he puts a vast deal of activity out to interest, and receives a large measure of nervous derangement in return. Either he absents himself entirely from all fellowship, and lives a recluse in a garret, with carpet slippers and a leaden inkpot; or he comes among people swiftly and bitterly, in a contraction of his whole nervous system, to discharge some temper before he returns to work. I do not care how much or how well he works, this fellow is an evil feature in other people's lives. They would be happier if he were dead. They could easier do without his services in the Circumlocution Office, than they can tolerate his fractious spirits. He poisons life at the well-head. It is better to be beggared out of hand by a scapegrace nephew, than daily hag-ridden by a peevish uncle.

And what, in God's name, is all this pother[31] about? For what cause do they embitter their own and other people's lives? That a man should publish three or thirty articles a year, that he should finish or not finish his great allegorical picture, are questions of little interest to the world. The ranks of life are full; and although a thousand fall, there are always some to go into the breach. When they told Joan of Arc[32] she should be at home minding women's work, she answered there were plenty to spin and wash. And so, even with your own rare gifts! When nature is "so careless of the

31. Fuss.
32. Joan of Arc (1412–1431) was a French peasant who believed that God had chosen her to lead the French army to victory against the English forces during the Hundred Years' War (1337–1453).

single life,"[33] why should we coddle ourselves into the fancy that our own is of exceptional importance? Suppose Shakespeare had been knocked on the head some dark night in Sir Thomas Lucy's[34] preserves, the world would have wagged on better or worse, the pitcher gone to the well, the scythe to the corn, and the student to his book; and no one been any the wiser of the loss. There are not many works extant, if you look the alternative all over, which are worth the price of a pound of tobacco to a man of limited means. This is a sobering reflection for the proudest of our earthly vanities. Even a tobacconist may, upon consideration, find no great cause for personal vainglory in the phrase; for although tobacco is an admirable sedative, the qualities necessary for retailing it are neither rare nor precious in themselves. Alas and alas! you may take it how you will, but the services of no single individual are indispensable. Atlas[35] was just a gentleman with a protracted nightmare! And yet you see merchants who go and labour themselves into a great fortune and thence into the bankruptcy court; scribblers who keep scribbling at little articles until their temper is a cross to all who come about them, as though Pharaoh should set the Israelites to make a pin instead of a pyramid; and fine young men who work themselves into a decline, and are driven off in a hearse with white plumes upon it. Would you not suppose these persons had been whispered, by the Master of the Ceremonies, the promise of some momentous destiny? and that this lukewarm bullet on which they play their farces was the bull's-eye and

---

33. From Tennyson's *In Memoriam A.H.H.* (1849):

> Are God and Nature then at strife,
> That Nature lends such evil dreams?
> So careful of the type she seems,
> So careless of the single life (55.5-8)

34. The magistrate Thomas Lucy (1532–1600) was embroiled in a bitter feud with Shakespeare and his family. Tempers flared when Shakespeare began poaching game from Lucy's estate.

35. In Greek mythology, Atlas is a Titan condemned by Zeus to hold up the sky for eternity.

centrepoint of all the universe? And yet it is not so. The ends for which they give away their priceless youth, for all they know, may be chimerical or hurtful; the glory and riches they expect may never come, or may find them indifferent; and they and the world they inhabit are so inconsiderable that the mind freezes at the thought.

PAN'S PIPES

The world in which we live has been variously said and sung by the most ingenious poets and philosophers: these reducing it to formulae and chemical ingredients, those striking the lyre in high-sounding measures for the handiwork of God. What experience supplies is of a mingled tissue, and the choosing mind has much to reject before it can get together the materials of a theory. Dew and thunder, destroying Attila[1] and the Spring lambkins, belong to an order of contrasts which no repetition can assimilate. There is an uncouth, outlandish strain throughout the web of the world, as from a vexatious planet in the house of life. Things are not congruous and wear strange disguises: the consummate flower is fostered out of dung, and after nourishing itself awhile with heaven's delicate distillations, decays again into indistinguishable soil; and with Caesar's ashes, Hamlet tells us, the urchins make dirt pies

1. Attila the Hun (c.406–453), nomadic ruler of the Hunnic Empire and enemy of the Eastern and Western Roman Empires.

and filthily besmear their countenance.[2] Nay, the kindly shine of summer, when tracked home with the scientific spyglass, is found to issue from the most portentous nightmare of the universe—the great, conflagrant sun: a world of hell's squibs,[3] tumultuary, roaring aloud, inimical to life. The sun itself is enough to disgust a human being of the scene which he inhabits; and you would not fancy there was a green or habitable spot in a universe thus awfully lighted up. And yet it is by the blaze of such a conflagration, to which the fire of Rome was but a spark, that we do all our fiddling,[4] and hold domestic tea-parties at the arbour door.

The Greeks figured Pan, the god of Nature, now terribly stamping his foot, so that armies were dispersed; now by the woodside on a summer noon trolling on his pipe until he charmed the hearts of upland ploughmen. And the Greeks, in so figuring, uttered the last word of human experience. To certain smoke-dried spirits matter and motion and elastic æthers, and the hypothesis of this or that other spectacled professor, tell a speaking[5] story; but for youth and all ductile and congenial minds, Pan is not dead, but of all the classic hierarchy alone survives in triumph; goat-footed, with a gleeful and an angry look, the type of the shaggy world:

---

2. Stevenson appears to be confusing a passage in *Hamlet* (c.1602) with one in Dickens's *The Mystery of Edwin Drood* (1870), published eight years before "Pan's Pipes." Dickens describes the old "Cathedral town" of Cloisterham: "the Cloisterham children grow small salad in the dust of abbots and abbesses, and make dirt-pies of nuns and friars." In Shakespeare's play, by contrast, Hamlet asks, "Why may not imagination trace the noble dust of / Alexander till 'a find it stopping a bunghole?" (5.1.205–6). He continues:

> Imperious Caesar, dead and turned to clay,
> Might stop a hole to keep the wind away.
> O, that that earth which kept the world in awe
> Should patch a wall t' expel the winter's flaw! (5.1.215–18)

3. Fireworks.
4. During the Great Fire of Rome in AD 64, twenty-six-year-old Emperor Nero (AD 37 – AD 68) reportedly played the fiddle (or the lyre) while the city burned. The expression "to fiddle while Rome burns" means to behave frivolously in the face of crisis.
5. Faithful; accurate.

and in every wood, if you go with a spirit properly prepared, you shall hear the note of his pipe.

For it is a shaggy world, and yet studded with gardens; where the salt and tumbling sea receives clear rivers running from among reeds and lilies; fruitful and austere; a rustic world; sunshiny, lewd, and cruel. What is it the birds sing among the trees in pairing time? What means the sound of the rain falling far and wide upon the leafy forest? To what tune does the fisherman whistle, as he hauls in his net at morning, and the bright fish are heaped inside the boat? These are all airs upon Pan's pipe; he it was who gave them breath in the exultation of his heart, and gleefully modulated their outflow with his lips and fingers. The coarse mirth of herdsmen, shaking the dells with laughter and striking out high echoes from the rock; the tune of moving feet in the lamplit city, or on the smooth ballroom floor; the hooves of many horses, beating the wide pastures in alarm; the song of hurrying rivers; the colour of clear skies; and smiles and the live touch of hands; and the voice of things, and their significant look, and the renovating influence they breathe forth—these are his joyful measures, to which the whole earth treads in choral harmony. To this music the young lambs bound as to a tabor,[6] and the London shop-girl skips rudely in the dance. For it puts a spirit of gladness in all hearts; and to look on the happy side of nature is common, in their hours, to all created things. Some are vocal under a good influence, are pleasing whenever they are pleased, and hand on their happiness to others, as a child who, looking upon lovely things, looks lovely. Some leap to the strains with unapt foot, and make a halting figure in the universal dance. And some, like sour spectators at the play, receive the music into their hearts with an unmoved countenance, and walk like strangers through the general rejoicing. But let him feign never so carefully, there is not a man but has his pulses

6. Small drum.

shaken when Pan trolls out a stave of ecstasy and sets the world a-singing.

Alas if that were all! But oftentimes the air is changed; and in the screech of the night wind chasing navies, subverting the tall ships and the rooted cedar of the hills; in the random deadly levin[7] or the fury of headlong floods, we recognize the "dread foundation"[8] of life and the anger in Pan's heart. Earth wages open war against her children, and under her softest touch hides treacherous claws. The cool waters invite us in to drown; the domestic hearth burns up in the hour of sleep, and makes an end of all. Everything is good or bad, helpful or deadly, not in itself, but by its circumstances. For a few bright days in England the hurricane must break forth and the North Sea pay a toll of populous ships. And when the universal music has led lovers into the paths of dalliance, confident of Nature's sympathy, suddenly the air shifts into a minor,[9] and death makes a clutch from his ambuscade[10] below the bed of marriage. For death is given in a kiss; the dearest kindnesses are fatal; and into this life, where one thing preys upon another, the child too often makes its entrance from the mother's corpse. It is no wonder, with so traitorous a scheme of things, if the wise people who created for us the idea of Pan thought that of all fears the fear of him was the most terrible, since it embraces all. And still we preserve the phrase: a panic terror. To reckon dangers too curiously, to hearken too intently for the threat that runs through all the winning music of the world, to hold back the hand from the rose because of the thorn, and from life

7. Lightning.

8. An allusion to Wordsworth's sonnet "In My Mind's Eye a Temple, like a Cloud" (1827):

> And Love her towers of dread foundation laid
> Under the grave of things; Hope had her spire
> Star-high, and pointing still to something higher (10–12)

9. A minor key.

10. Ambush.

because of death: this it is to be afraid of Pan. Highly respectable citizens who flee life's pleasures and responsibilities and keep, with upright hat, upon the midway of custom, avoiding the right hand and the left, the ecstasies and the agonies, how surprised they would be if they could hear their attitude mythologically expressed, and knew themselves as tooth-chattering ones, who flee from Nature because they fear the hand of Nature's God! Shrilly sound Pan's pipes; and behold the banker instantly concealed in the bank parlour! For to distrust one's impulses is to be recreant[11] to Pan.

There are moments when the mind refuses to be satisfied with evolution, and demands a ruddier presentation of the sum of man's experience. Sometimes the mood is brought about by laughter at the humorous side of life, as when, abstracting ourselves from earth, we imagine people plodding on foot, or seated in ships and speedy trains, with the planet all the while whirling in the opposite direction, so that, for all their hurry, they travel back-foremost through the universe of space. Sometimes it comes by the spirit of delight, and sometimes by the spirit of terror. At least, there will always be hours when we refuse to be put off by the feint of explanation, nicknamed science; and demand instead some palpitating image of our estate, that shall represent the troubled and uncertain element in which we dwell, and satisfy reason by the means of art. Science writes of the world as if with the cold finger of a starfish; it is all true; but what is it when compared to the reality of which it discourses? where hearts beat high in April, and death strikes, and hills totter in the earthquake, and there is a glamour over all the objects of sight, and a thrill in all noises for the ear, and Romance herself has made her dwelling among men? So we come back to the old myth, and hear the goat-footed piper making the music which is itself the charm and terror of things; and when a glen invites our visiting footsteps, fancy that Pan leads

11. A traitor.

us thither with a gracious tremolo;[12] or when our hearts quail at the thunder of the cataract, tell ourselves that he has stamped his hoof in the nigh thicket.

12. A tremulous or wavering musical tone used to express emotion.

ÆS TRIPLEX

The changes wrought by death are in themselves so sharp and final, and so terrible and melancholy in their consequences, that the thing stands alone in man's experience, and has no parallel upon earth. It outdoes all other accidents because it is the last of them. Sometimes it leaps suddenly upon its victims, like a Thug;[1] sometimes it lays a regular siege and creeps upon their citadel during a score of years. And when the business is done, there is sore havoc made in other people's lives, and a pin knocked out by which many subsidiary friendships hung together. There are empty chairs, solitary walks, and single beds at night. Again, in taking away our friends, death does not take them away utterly, but leaves behind a mocking, tragical, and soon intolerable residue, which must be hurriedly concealed. Hence a whole chapter of sights and customs striking to the mind, from the pyramids of Egypt to the gibbets and dule trees[2] of mediæval Europe. The poorest persons have a bit of pageant going towards the tomb;

1. The English word "thug" derives from the Hindi word *thag* ("deceiver") and refers to an Indian religious cult that claimed thousands of lives annually in early-nineteenth-century India. Thugs robbed and strangled wayfarers along trade routes, sacrificing them to the Hindu goddess Kali. In the name of eradicating Thuggee, the British tightened their administrative grip on the subcontinent, presenting themselves as guarantors of political and economic stability.
2. The hanging-tree, or tree of lamentation, where the corpses of criminals were displayed.

memorial stones are set up over the least memorable; and, in order to preserve some show of respect for what remains of our old loves and friendships, we must accompany it with much grimly ludicrous ceremonial, and the hired undertaker parades before the door. All this, and much more of the same sort, accompanied by the eloquence of poets, has gone a great way to put humanity in error; nay, in many philosophies the error has been embodied and laid down with every circumstance of logic; although in real life the bustle and swiftness, in leaving people little time to think, have not left them time enough to go dangerously wrong in practice.

As a matter of fact, although few things are spoken of with more fearful whisperings than this prospect of death, few have less influence on conduct under healthy circumstances. We have all heard of cities in South America built upon the side of fiery mountains, and how, even in this tremendous neighbourhood, the inhabitants are not a jot more impressed by the solemnity of mortal conditions than if they were delving[3] gardens in the greenest corner of England. There are serenades and suppers and much gallantry among the myrtles overhead; and meanwhile the foundation shudders underfoot, the bowels of the mountain growl, and at any moment living ruin may leap sky-high into the moonlight, and tumble man and his merry-making in the dust. In the eyes of very young people, and very dull old ones, there is something indescribably reckless and desperate in such a picture. It seems not credible that respectable married people, with umbrellas, should find appetite for a bit of supper within quite a long distance of a fiery mountain; ordinary life begins to smell of high-handed debauch when it is carried on so close to a catastrophe; and even cheese and salad, it seems, could hardly be relished in such circumstances without something like a defiance of the Creator. It should be a place for nobody but hermits

3. Digging.

dwelling in prayer and maceration, or mere born-devils drowning care in a perpetual carouse.

And yet, when one comes to think upon it calmly, the situation of these South American citizens forms only a very pale figure for the state of ordinary mankind. This world itself, travelling blindly and swiftly in overcrowded space, among a million other worlds travelling blindly and swiftly in contrary directions, may very well come by a knock that would set it into explosion like a penny squib.[4] And what, pathologically looked at, is the human body with all its organs, but a mere bagful of petards?[5] The least of these is as dangerous to the whole economy as the ship's powder-magazine to the ship; and with every breath we breathe, and every meal we eat, we are putting one or more of them in peril. If we clung as devotedly as some philosophers pretend we do to the abstract idea of life, or were half as frightened as they make out we are, for the subversive accident that ends it all, the trumpets might sound by the hour and no one would follow them into battle—the blue-peter[6] might fly at the truck,[7] but who would climb into a sea-going ship? Think (if these philosophers were right) with what a preparation of spirit we should affront the daily peril of the dinner-table: a deadlier spot than any battlefield in history; where the far greater proportion of our ancestors have miserably left their bones! What woman would ever be lured into marriage, so much more dangerous than the wildest sea? And what would it be to grow old? For, after a certain distance, every step we take in life we find the ice growing thinner below our feet, and all around us and behind us we see our contemporaries going through. By the time a man gets well into the seventies, his continued existence is a mere miracle; and when he lays his old bones in bed for the night, there is an overwhelming probability

4. Cheap firecracker.
5. Small bombs.
6. A nautical signal flag (blue with a white square) signifying "all aboard."
7. The cap at the top of a ship's mast from which signal flags are flown.

that he will never see the day. Do the old men mind it, as a matter of fact? Why, no. They were never merrier; they have their grog at night, and tell the raciest stories; they hear of the death of people about their own age, or even younger, not as if it was a grisly warning, but with a simple childlike pleasure at having outlived someone else; and when a draught might puff them out like a guttering candle, or a bit of a stumble shatter them like so much glass, their old hearts keep sound and unaffrighted, and they go on, bubbling with laughter, through years of man's age compared to which the valley at Balaklava[8] was as safe and peaceful as a village cricket-green on Sunday. It may fairly be questioned (if we look to the peril only) whether it was a much more daring feat for Curtius to plunge into the gulf,[9] than for any old gentleman of ninety to doff his clothes and clamber into bed.

Indeed, it is a memorable subject for consideration, with what unconcern and gaiety mankind pricks on along the Valley of the Shadow of Death. The whole way is one wilderness of snares, and the end of it, for those who fear the last pinch, is irrevocable ruin. And yet we go spinning through it all, like a party for the Derby.[10] Perhaps the reader remembers one of the humorous devices of the deified Caligula:[11] how he encouraged a vast concourse of holiday-makers on to his bridge over Baiæ bay;[12] and when they were in the height of their enjoyment, turned loose the Prætorian

8. The Battle of Balaclava occurred on October 25, 1854 in the Crimean War (1853–56) and marked a rare victory for Russia against the allied forces of Great Britain, France and the Ottoman Empire. Tennyson's poem "The Charge of the Light Brigade" (1854) commemorates the British soldiers who lost their lives that day, when the British light cavalry charged the Russian artillerymen.
9. In Roman mythology, the soldier Marcus Curtius sacrificed himself to appease the angry gods, riding his horse into a giant sinkhole that formed in the center of Rome after an earthquake.
10. An annual horse race run at Epsom Downs in Surrey, England.
11. The Roman emperor Caius Caligula (AD 12 – AD 41), notorious for his debauchery, cruelty and eccentricity, declared himself a living god.
12. Caligula ordered the construction of a three-mile-long floating bridge across this bay on the Gulf of Naples, so that he might ride his horse across.

guards[13] among the company, and had them tossed into the sea. This is no bad miniature of the dealings of nature with the transitory race of man. Only, what a chequered picnic we have of it, even while it lasts! and into what great waters, not to be crossed by any swimmer, God's pale Prætorian throws us over in the end!

We live the time that a match flickers; we pop the cork of a ginger-beer bottle, and the earthquake swallows us on the instant. Is it not odd, is it not incongruous, is it not, in the highest sense of human speech, incredible, that we should think so highly of the ginger-beer, and regard so little the devouring earthquake? The love of Life and the fear of Death are two famous phrases that grow harder to understand the more we think about them. It is a well-known fact that an immense proportion of boat accidents would never happen if people held the sheet[14] in their hands instead of making it fast; and yet, unless it be some martinet of a professional mariner or some landsman with shattered nerves, every one of God's creatures makes it fast. A strange instance of man's unconcern and brazen boldness in the face of death!

We confound ourselves with metaphysical phrases, which we import into daily talk with noble inappropriateness. We have no idea of what death is, apart from its circumstances and some of its consequences to others; and although we have some experience of living, there is not a man on earth who has flown so high into abstraction as to have any practical guess at the meaning of the word *life*. All literature, from Job and Omar Khayam to Thomas Carlyle or Walt Whitman,[15] is but an attempt to look upon the human state with such largeness of view as shall enable us to rise

13. The elite forces who guarded the emperor.
14. The rope or cable used to control the corners of the sail.
15. The Old Testament Book of Job tells of the various trials that befell the prophet; Omar Khayyám (1048–1131) was a Persian poet and mathematician whose poetic meditation upon the impermanence of life was translated by Victorian poet Edward Fitzgerald (1809–1883); Thomas Carlyle (1795–1881), Scottish philosopher, historian and essayist, left an indelible mark on Victorian culture by questioning the utilitarianism and unbridled materialism unleashed by the Industrial Revolution; Walt Whitman (1819–1892), American poet and pioneer of free verse, infused his

from the consideration of living to the Definition of Life. And our sages give us about the best satisfaction in their power when they say that it is a vapour, or a show, or made out of the same stuff with dreams.[16] Philosophy, in its more rigid sense, has been at the same work for ages; and after a myriad bald heads have wagged over the problem, and piles of words have been heaped one upon another into dry and cloudy volumes without end, philosophy has the honour of laying before us, with modest pride, her contribution towards the subject: that life is a Permanent Possibility of Sensation.[17] Truly a fine result! A man may very well love beef, or hunting, or a woman; but surely, surely, not a Permanent Possibility of Sensation! He may be afraid of a precipice, or a dentist, or a large enemy with a club, or even an undertaker's man; but not certainly of abstract death. We may trick[18] with the word life in its dozen senses until we are weary of tricking; we may argue in terms of all the philosophies on earth, but one fact remains true throughout—that we do not love life, in the sense that we are greatly preoccupied about its conservation; that we do not, properly speaking, love life at all, but living. Into the views of the least careful there will enter some degree of providence; no man's eyes are fixed entirely on the passing hour; but although we have some anticipation of good health, good weather, wine, active employment, love, and self-approval, the sum of these anticipations does not amount to anything like a general view of life's possibilities and issues; nor are those who cherish them most vividly at all the most scrupulous of their personal safety. To be deeply interested in the accidents of our existence, to enjoy

---

masterpiece *Leaves of Grass* (1855) with his vagabond spirit and openness to new experience.

16. From Shakespeare's *The Tempest* (1610–11): "We are such stuff / As dreams are made on, and our little life / Is rounded with a sleep" (4.1.156–58).

17. In his *An Examination of Sir William Hamilton's Philosophy* (1865), utilitarian philosopher John Stuart Mill (1806–1873) famously defined matter as the "permanent possibility of sensation."

18. Fool.

keenly the mixed texture of human experience, rather leads a man to disregard precautions, and risk his neck against a straw. For surely the love of living is stronger in an Alpine climber roping over a peril, or a hunter riding merrily at a stiff fence, than in a creature who lives upon a diet and walks a measured distance in the interest of his constitution.

There is a great deal of very vile nonsense talked upon both sides of the matter: tearing divines[19] reducing life to the dimensions of a mere funeral procession, so short as to be hardly decent; and melancholy unbelievers yearning for the tomb as if it were a world too far away. Both sides must feel a little ashamed of their performances now and again when they draw in their chairs to dinner. Indeed, a good meal and a bottle of wine is an answer to most standard works upon the question. When a man's heart warms to his viands, he forgets a great deal of sophistry, and soars into a rosy zone of contemplation. Death may be knocking at the door, like the Commander's statue;[20] we have something else in hand, thank God, and let him knock. Passing-bells[21] are ringing all the world over. All the world over, and every hour, someone is parting company with all his aches and ecstasies. For us also the trap is laid. But we are so fond of life that we have no leisure to entertain the terror of death. It is a honeymoon with us all through, and none of the longest. Small blame to us if we give our whole hearts to this glowing bride of ours, to the appetites, to honour, to the hungry curiosity of the mind, to the pleasure of the eyes in nature, and the pride of our own nimble bodies.

We all of us appreciate the sensations; but as for caring about the Permanence of the Possibility, a man's head is generally very

---

19. Theologians.
20. An allusion to the legend of Don Juan: a libertine who seduces numerous women and kills the father of one. Depending on the telling, Don Juan either invites a statue of the murdered man to dinner, or he accepts the statue's invitation to dine. In a final confrontation between the wily Juan and the paternal statue, the libertine is sent to hell.
21. Funeral bells.

bald,[22] and his senses very dull, before he comes to that. Whether we regard life as a lane leading to a dead wall—a mere bag's end,[23] as the French say—or whether we think of it as a vestibule or gymnasium, where we wait our turn and prepare our faculties for some more noble destiny; whether we thunder in a pulpit, or pule in little atheistic poetry-books, about its vanity and brevity; whether we look justly for years of health and vigour, or are about to mount into a bath-chair,[24] as a step towards the hearse; in each and all of these views and situations there is but one conclusion possible: that a man should stop his ears against paralyzing terror, and run the race that is set before him with a single mind. No one surely could have recoiled with more heartache and terror from the thought of death than our respected lexicographer;[25] and yet we know how little it affected his conduct, how wisely and boldly he walked, and in what a fresh and lively vein he spoke of life. Already an old man, he ventured on his Highland tour;[26] and his heart, bound with triple brass,[27] did not recoil before twenty-seven individual cups of tea. As courage and intelligence are the two qualities best worth a good man's cultivation, so it is the first part of intelligence to recognize our precarious estate in life, and the first part of courage to be not at all abashed before the fact. A frank and somewhat headlong carriage, not looking too

22. John Stuart Mill was very bald.
23. A cul-de-sac; literally, "bottom of the bag."
24. A hooded wheelchair, or rolling chaise, which originated in the English spa town of Bath.
25. Samuel Johnson (See "An Apology for Idlers.").
26. In 1773, at sixty-three, Johnson toured the Scottish Highlands and outer islands with his friend Boswell. Two years later, Johnson published *A Journey to the Western Islands of Scotland.*
27. The title of this essay—"Triple Brass"—is an allusion to Roman poet Horace (65 BC – 8 BC). In *Odes,* Horace marvels at the fearlessness of early seafarers: "*illi robur et aes triplex / circa pectus erat, qui fragilem truci / commisit pelago ratem / primus*" (1.3.9–12). Translation: "Oak and triple bands of brass circled the breast of the man who first entrusted his fragile craft to the ferocious open sea." Here, the heart of the sailor, encased in rib and muscle, and the "breast" of the brass-encircled vessel function as metaphors for each other. The man's very fragility is what makes his willingness to conquer the ocean so "brassy."

anxiously before, not dallying in maudlin regret over the past, stamps the man who is well armoured for this world.

And not only well armoured for himself, but a good friend and a good citizen to boot. We do not go to cowards for tender dealing; there is nothing so cruel as panic; the man who has least fear for his own carcase[28] has most time to consider others. That eminent chemist[29] who took his walks abroad in tin shoes, and subsisted wholly upon tepid milk, had all his work cut out for him in considerate dealings with his own digestion. So soon as prudence has begun to grow up in the brain, like a dismal fungus, it finds its first expression in a paralysis of generous acts. The victim begins to shrink spiritually; he develops a fancy for parlours with a regulated temperature, and takes his morality on the principle of tin shoes and tepid milk. The care of one important body or soul becomes so engrossing, that all the noises of the outer world begin to come thin and faint into the parlour with the regulated temperature; and the tin shoes go equably forward over blood and rain. To be overwise is to ossify; and the scruple-monger ends by standing stockstill. Now the man who has his heart on his sleeve, and a good whirling weathercock of a brain, who reckons his life as a thing to be dashingly used and cheerfully hazarded, makes a very different acquaintance of the world, keeps all his pulses going true and fast, and gathers impetus as he runs, until, if he be running towards anything better than wildfire, he may shoot up and become a constellation in the end. Lord look after his health, Lord have a care of his soul, says he; and he has at the key of the position, and swashes through incongruity and peril towards his aim. Death is on all sides of him with pointed batteries, as he is on all sides of all of us; unfortunate surprises gird him round; mim-mouthed[30] friends and relations hold up their hands in quite a little elegiacal synod about his path: and what cares he for all this? Being a true

28. Carcass.
29. A local Edinburgh pharmacist who had a fear of catching cold.
30. Prim; affectedly reserved.

lover of living, a fellow with something pushing and spontaneous in his inside, he must, like any other soldier, in any other stirring, deadly warfare, push on at his best pace until he touch the goal. "A peerage or Westminster Abbey!" cried Nelson[31] in his bright, boyish, heroic manner. These are great incentives; not for any of these, but for the plain satisfaction of living, of being about their business in some sort or other, do the brave, serviceable men of every nation tread down the nettle danger, and pass flyingly over all the stumbling-blocks of prudence. Think of the heroism of Johnson, think of that superb indifference to mortal limitation that set him upon his dictionary,[32] and carried him through triumphantly until the end! Who, if he were wisely considerate of things at large, would ever embark upon any work much more considerable than a halfpenny postcard? Who would project a serial novel, after Thackeray and Dickens had each fallen in midcourse?[33] Who would find heart enough to begin to live, if he dallied with the consideration of death?

And, after all, what sorry and pitiful quibbling all this is? To forego all the issues of living in a parlour with a regulated temperature—as if that were not to die a hundred times over, and for ten years at a stretch! As if it were not to die in one's own lifetime, and without even the sad immunities of death! As if it were not to die, and yet be the patient spectators of our own pitiable change! The Permanent Possibility is preserved, but the sensations carefully held at arm's length, as if one kept a photographic plate in a dark chamber. It is better to lose health like a spendthrift than to

---

31. Lord Horatio Nelson (1758–1805), British admiral and naval hero of the Revolutionary and Napoleonic Wars, is reported to have declared on the eve of the Battle of the Nile (1798), "Before this time tomorrow, I shall have gained a peerage, or Westminster Abbey," meaning he would either survive and receive a hereditary title, or he would die heroically and be buried in London at the cathedral Westminster, alongside kings, queens and national heroes.

32. Johnson's greatest achievement was his monumental 42,773-entry *A Dictionary of the English Language* (1755).

33. Both Thackeray and Dickens died before completing their final novels: *Denis Duval* (1863) and *The Mystery of Edwin Drood* (1870), respectively.

waste it like a miser. It is better to live and be done with it, than to die daily in the sick-room. By all means begin your folio; even if the doctor does not give you a year, even if he hesitates about a month, make one brave push and see what can be accomplished in a week. It is not only in finished undertakings that we ought to honour useful labour. A spirit goes out of the man who means execution, which outlives the most untimely ending. All who have meant good work with their whole hearts, have done good work, although they may die before they have the time to sign it. Every heart that has beat strong and cheerfully has left a hopeful impulse behind it in the world, and bettered the tradition of mankind. And even if death catch people, like an open pitfall, and in mid-career, laying out vast projects, and planning monstrous foundations, flushed with hope, and their mouths full of boastful language, they[34] should be at once tripped up and silenced: is there not something brave and spirited in such a termination? and does not life go down with a better grace, foaming in full body over a precipice, than miserably straggling to an end in sandy deltas? When the Greeks made their fine saying that those whom the gods love die young, I cannot help believing they had this sort of death also in their eye. For surely, at whatever age it overtake the man, this is to die young. Death has not been suffered to take so much as an illusion from his heart. In the hot-fit of life, a-tiptoe on the highest point of being, he passes at a bound on to the other side. The noise of the mallet and chisel is scarcely quenched, the trumpets are hardly done blowing, when, trailing with him clouds of glory,[35] this happy-starred, full-blooded spirit shoots into the spiritual land.

---

34. Stevenson probably meant to include an "and" before "they."

35. An allusion to Wordsworth's "Ode: Intimations of Immortality from Recollections of Early Childhood" (1807):

> Not in entire forgetfulness,
> And not in utter nakedness,
> But trailing clouds of glory do we come
> From God, who is our home:
> Heaven lies about us in our infancy! (63–66)

THE EDUCATION OF AN ENGINEER

Anstruther[1] is a place sacred to the Muse;[2] she inspired (really to a considerable extent) Tennant's vernacular poem "Anster Fair";[3] and I have there waited upon her myself with much devotion. This was when I came as a young man to glean engineering experience from the building of the breakwater.[4] What I gleaned, I am sure I do not know; but indeed I had already my own private determination to be an author; I loved the art of words and the appearances of life; and *travellers,*[5] and *headers,*[6] and *rubble,*[7] and *polished ashlar,*[8] and *pierres perdues,*[9] and even the thrilling question of the *string-course,*[10] interested me only (if they interested me at all) as properties for some possible romance or as words to add to my vocabulary. To grow a little

1. A fishing village on the east coast of Scotland.
2. Presumably Thalia, Muse of comedy. In Greek mythology, the Muses were goddesses of inspiration, each associated with an artistic or intellectual endeavor: astronomy, epic poetry, dance, history, lyric poetry, tragedy, etc. Mount Helicon, Mount Olympus and Mount Parnassus were among the locations sacred to the Muses.
3. William Tennant (1784–1848), native of Anstruther, published his comic poem in 1814, appealing to his Muse for help glorifying "Anster's turnip-bearing vales."
4. Sea wall or jetty.
5. Mechanisms for moving, lifting or sliding construction materials around a site.
6. Bricks or stone blocks placed with their ends to the face of the wall.
7. Rough pieces of undressed stone used to fill cavities in walls.
8. Finely cut stones used as facing on walls.
9. Blocks of stone or concrete piled loosely in the water to form a seawall foundation.
10. A raised horizontal band of bricks or stone on a structure.

catholic is the compensation of years; youth is one-eyed; and in those days, though I haunted the breakwater by day, and even loved the place for the sake of the sunshine, the thrilling seaside air, the wash of waves on the sea-face, the green glimmer of the divers' helmets far below, and the musical chinking of the masons, my one genuine preoccupation lay elsewhere, and my only industry was in the hours when I was not on duty. I lodged with a certain Bailie Brown, a carpenter by trade; and there, as soon as dinner was despatched, in a chamber scented with dry rose-leaves, drew in my chair to the table and proceeded to pour forth literature, at such a speed, and with such intimations of early death and immortality,[11] as I now look back upon with wonder. Then it was that I wrote "Voces Fidelium,"[12] a series of dramatic monologues in verse; then that I indited[13] the bulk of a covenanting novel[14]—like so many others, never finished. Late I sat into the night, toiling (as I thought) under the very dart of death,[15] toiling to leave a memory behind me. I feel moved to thrust aside the curtain of the years, to hail that poor feverish idiot, to bid him go to bed and clap "Voces Fidelium" on the fire before he goes; so clear does he appear before me, sitting there between his candles in the rose-scented room and the late night; so ridiculous a picture (to my elderly wisdom) does the fool

11. A self-deprecating allusion to Wordsworth's "Intimations of Immortality."
12. Voices of the Faithful.
13. Wrote.
14. Inspired by Walter Scott's *Old Mortality* (1816) and James Hogg's *The Brownie of Bodsbeck* (1818), Stevenson's unfinished novel was set in seventeenth-century Scotland, when the Covenanters, a nationalist Presbyterian protest movement, became the dominant force in Scottish politics, their ascendancy fueled by resistance to religious reforms imposed by the English. In 1866, however, Stevenson did publish his research for the novel in the form of a lengthy historical essay: *The Pentland Rising: A Page of History, 1666*.
15. See Shakespeare's *Cymbeline* (1611):

> Stark, as you see,
> Thus smiling, as some fly had tickled slumber,
> Not as Death's dart being laughed at; his cheek
> Reposing on a cushion. (4.2.209–12)

present! But he was driven to his bed at last without miraculous intervention; and the manner of his driving sets the last touch upon this eminently youthful business. The weather was then so warm that I must keep the windows open; the night without was populous with moths. As the late darkness deepened, my literary tapers beaconed forth more brightly; thicker and thicker came the dusty night-fliers, to gyrate for one brilliant instant round the flame and fall in agonies upon my paper. Flesh and blood could not endure the spectacle; to capture immortality was doubtless a noble enterprise, but not to capture it at such a cost of suffering; and out would go the candles, and off would I go to bed in the darkness, raging to think that the blow might fall on the morrow, and there was "Voces Fidelium" still incomplete. Well, the moths are all gone, and "Voces Fidelium" along with them; only the fool is still on hand and practises new follies.

Only one thing in connection with the harbour tempted me, and that was the diving, an experience I burned to taste of. But this was not to be, at least in Anstruther; and the subject involves a change of scene to the subarctic town of Wick.[16] You can never have dwelt in a country more unsightly than that part of Caithness,[17] the land faintly swelling, faintly falling, not a tree, not a hedgerow, the fields divided by single slate stones set upon their edge, the wind always singing in your ears and (down the long road that led nowhere) thrumming in the telegraph wires. Only as you approached the coast was there anything to stir the heart. The plateau broke down to the North Sea in formidable cliffs, the tall out-stacks[18] rose like pillars ringed about with surf, the coves were over-brimmed with clamorous froth, the sea-birds screamed, the wind sang in the thyme on the cliff's edge; here and there, small ancient castles toppled on the brim; here and there, it was possible to dip into a dell of shelter, where

16. Town in the far north of Scotland.
17. County in northern Scotland.
18. Rocky outcrops off a coast.

you might lie and tell yourself you were a little warm, and hear (near at hand) the whin-pods[19] bursting in the afternoon sun, and (farther off) the rumour of the turbulent sea. As for Wick itself, it is one of the meanest of man's towns, and situate certainly on the baldest of God's bays. It lives for herring, and a strange sight it is to see (of an afternoon) the heights of Pulteney blackened by seaward-looking fishers, as when a city crowds to a review—or, as when bees have swarmed, the ground is horrible with lumps and clusters; and a strange sight, and a beautiful, to see the fleet put silently out against a rising moon, the sea-line rough as a wood with sails, and ever and again and one after another, a boat flitting swiftly by the silver disk. This mass of fishers, this great fleet of boats, is out of all proportion to the town itself; and the oars are manned and the nets hauled by immigrants from the Long Island (as we call the outer Hebrides),[20] who come for that season only, and depart again, if "the take" be poor, leaving debts behind them. In a bad year, the end of the herring fishery is therefore an exciting time; fights are common, riots often possible; an apple knocked from a child's hand was once the signal for something like a war; and even when I was there, a gunboat lay in the bay to assist the authorities. To contrary interests, it should be observed, the curse of Babel[21] is here added: the Lews men are Gaelic speakers, those of Caithness have adopted English; an odd circumstance, if you reflect that both must be largely Norsemen by descent. I remember seeing one of the strongest instances of this division: a thing like a Punch-and-Judy box erected on the flat gravestones of the churchyard; from the hutch or proscenium—I know not what to call it—an

19. The seedpods of spiny gorse.
20. Island chain off the west coast of Scotland.
21. The curse of Babel is the inability to comprehend what other people are saying. In the Book of Genesis, a wrathful God renders human speech incomprehensible, frustrating their efforts to work together on an engineering marvel: the construction of a tower that would reach to heaven. God's alienated children scatter to the four corners of the earth to hone their babble into tribal languages.

eldritch-looking[22] preacher laying down the law in Gaelic about someone of the name of *Powl*, whom I at last divined to be the apostle to the Gentiles;[23] a large congregation of the Lews men very devoutly listening; and on the outskirts of the crowd, some of the town's children (to whom the whole affair was Greek and Hebrew) profanely playing tigg.[24] The same descent, the same country, the same narrow sect of the same religion, and all these bonds made very largely nugatory by an accidental difference of dialect!

Into the bay of Wick stretched the dark length of the unfinished breakwater, in its cage of open staging; the travellers (like frames of churches) over-plumbing all; and away at the extreme end, the divers toiling unseen on the foundation. On a platform of loose planks, the assistants turned their air-mills;[25] a stone might be swinging between wind and water; underneath the swell ran gaily; and from time to time, a mailed[26] dragon with a window-glass snout came dripping up the ladder. Youth is a blessed season after all; my stay at Wick was in the year of "Voces Fidelium" and the rose-leaf room at Bailie Brown's; and already I did not care two straws for literary glory. Posthumous ambition perhaps requires an atmosphere of roses; and the more rugged excitant of Wick east winds had made another boy of me. To go down in the diving-dress, that was my absorbing fancy; and with the countenance of a certain handsome scamp of a diver, Bob Bain by name, I gratified the whim.

It was grey, harsh, easterly weather, the swell ran pretty high, and out in the open there were "skipper's daughters,"[27] when I found myself at last on the diver's platform, twenty pounds of lead upon each foot and my whole person swollen with ply and

22. Weird-looking.
23. Paul.
24. Tag.
25. A manually operated pump that supplies air to the diver's helmet through a hose.
26. Clad in armor.
27. Waves with white crests.

ply of woollen underclothing. One moment, the salt wind was whistling round my night-capped head; the next, I was crushed almost double under the weight of the helmet. As that intolerable burthen was laid upon me, I could have found it in my heart (only for shame's sake) to cry off from the whole enterprise. But it was too late. The attendants began to turn the hurdy-gurdy,[28] and the air to whistle through the tube; someone screwed in the barred window of the vizor; and I was cut off in a moment from my fellow-men; standing there in their midst, but quite divorced from intercourse: a creature deaf and dumb, pathetically looking forth upon them from a climate of his own. Except that I could move and feel, I was like a man fallen in a catalepsy.[29] But time was scarce given me to realise my isolation; the weights were hung upon my back and breast, the signal-rope was thrust into my unresisting hand; and setting a twenty-pound foot upon the ladder, I began ponderously to descend.

Some twenty rounds[30] below the platform, twilight fell. Looking up, I saw a low green heaven mottled with vanishing bells of white; looking around, except for the weedy spokes and shafts of the ladder, nothing but a green gloaming, somewhat opaque but very restful and delicious. Thirty rounds lower, I stepped off on the *pierres perdues* of the foundation; a dumb helmeted figure took me by the hand, and made a gesture (as I read it) of encouragement; and looking in at the creature's window, I beheld the face of Bain. There we were, hand to hand and (when it pleased us) eye to eye; and either might have burst himself with shouting, and not a whisper come to his companion's hearing. Each, in his own little world of air, stood incommunicably separate.

Bob had told me ere this a little tale, a five minutes' drama at the bottom of the sea, which at that moment possibly shot across

28. A hurdy-gurdy is a stringed musical instrument with a hand crank. Stevenson is suggesting that the air-mill looks and sounds like a hurdy-gurdy.
29. Trance.
30. Rungs on a ladder.

my mind. He was down with another, settling a stone of the sea-wall. They had it well adjusted, Bob gave the signal, the scissors[31] were slipped, the stone set home; and it was time to turn to something else. But still his companion remained bowed over the block like a mourner on a tomb, or only raised himself to make absurd contortions and mysterious signs unknown to the vocabulary of the diver. There, then, these two stood for a while, like the dead and the living; till there flashed a fortunate thought into Bob's mind, and he stooped, peered through the window of that other world, and beheld the face of its inhabitant wet with streaming tears. Ah! the man was in pain! And Bob, glancing downward, saw what was the trouble: the block had been lowered on the foot of that unfortunate—he was caught alive at the bottom of the sea under fifteen tons of rock.

That two men should handle a stone so heavy, even swinging in the scissors, may appear strange to the inexpert. These must bear in mind the great density of the water of the sea, and the surprising results of transplantation to that medium. To understand a little what these are, and how a man's weight, so far from being an encumbrance, is the very ground of his agility, was the chief lesson of my submarine experience. The knowledge came upon me by degrees. As I began to go forward with the hand of my estranged companion, a world of tumbled stones was visible, pillared with the weedy uprights of the staging: overhead, a flat roof of green: a little in front, the sea-wall, like an unfinished rampart. And presently in our upward progress, Bob motioned me to leap upon a stone. I looked to see if he were possibly in earnest, and he only signed to me the more imperiously. Now the block stood six feet high; it would have been quite a leap to me unencumbered; with the breast and back weights, and the twenty pounds upon each foot, and the staggering load of the helmet, the thing was out of reason. I laughed aloud in my tomb; and to prove to Bob how

31. Grapple.

far he was astray, I gave a little impulse from my toes. Up I soared like a bird, my companion soaring at my side. As high as to the stone, and then higher, I pursued my impotent and empty flight. Even when the strong arm of Bob had checked my shoulders, my heels continued their ascent; so that I blew out sideways like an autumn leaf, and must be hauled in, hand over hand, as sailors haul in the slack of a sail, and propped upon my feet again like an intoxicated sparrow. Yet a little higher on the foundation, and we began to be affected by the bottom of the swell, running there like a strong breeze of wind. Or so I must suppose; for, safe in my cushion of air, I was conscious of no impact; only swayed idly like a weed, and was now borne helplessly abroad, and now swiftly—and yet with dream-like gentleness—impelled against my guide. So does a child's balloon divagate[32] upon the currents of the air, and touch and slide off again from every obstacle. So must have ineffectually swung, so resented their inefficiency, those light crowds that followed the Star of Hades,[33] and uttered exiguous voices in the land beyond Cocytus.[34]

There was something strangely exasperating, as well as strangely wearying, in these uncommanded evolutions. It is bitter to return to infancy, to be supported, and directed, and perpetually set upon your feet, by the hand of someone else. The air besides, as it is supplied to you by the busy millers on the platform, closes the eustachian tubes[35] and keeps the neophyte perpetually swallowing, till his throat is grown so dry that he can swallow no longer. And for all these reasons—although I had a fine, dizzy, muddle-headed joy in my surroundings, and longed, and tried, and always failed, to lay hands on the fish that darted here and there about me, swift as hummingbirds—yet I

32. Stray.
33. The Star of Hades is Lucifer or the "morning star," who falls from heaven with his defeated army of rebel angels: "the third part of the stars of heaven" (Revelation 12:4).
34. In Greek mythology, Cocytus is a river in the underworld.
35. The auditory tube linking the nasopharynx to the middle ear.

fancy I was rather relieved than otherwise when Bain brought me back to the ladder and signed to me to mount. And there was one more experience before me even then. Of a sudden, my ascending head passed into the trough of a swell. Out of the green, I shot at once into a glory of rosy, almost of sanguine light—the multitudinous seas incarnadined, the heaven above a vault of crimson. And then the glory faded into the hard, ugly daylight of a Caithness autumn, with a low sky, a grey sea, and a whistling wind.

Bob Bain had five shillings for his trouble, and I had done what I desired. It was one of the best things I got from my education as an engineer: of which, however, as a way of life, I wish to speak with sympathy. It takes a man into the open air; it keeps him hanging about harbour-sides, which is the richest form of idling; it carries him to wild islands; it gives him a taste of the genial dangers of the sea; it supplies him with dexterities to exercise; it makes demands upon his ingenuity; it will go far to cure him of any taste (if ever he had one) for the miserable life of cities. And when it has done so it carries him back and shuts him in an office! From the roaring skerry[36] and the wet thwart of the tossing boat, he passes to the stool and desk; and with a memory full of ships, and seas, and perilous headlands, and the shining pharos,[37] he must apply his long-sighted eyes to the petty niceties of drawing, or measure his inaccurate mind with several pages of consecutive figures. He is a wise youth, to be sure, who can balance one part of genuine life against two parts of drudgery between four walls, and for the sake of the one, manfully accept the other.

Wick was scarce an eligible place of stay. But how much better it was to hang in the cold wind upon the pier, to go down with Bob Bain among the roots of the staging, to be all day in

36. Rocky islet.
37. Lighthouse.

a boat coiling a wet rope and shouting orders—not always very wise—than to be warm and dry, and dull, and dead-alive, in the most comfortable office. And Wick itself had in those days a note of originality. It may have still, but I misdoubt it much. The old minister of Keiss[38] would not preach, in these degenerate times, for an hour and a half upon the clock. The gipsies must be gone from their cavern; where you might see, from the mouth, the women tending their fire, like Meg Merrilies,[39] and the men sleeping off their coarse potations; and where in winter gales, the surf would beleaguer them closely, bursting in their very door. A traveller today upon the Thurso coach[40] would scarce observe a little cloud of smoke among the moorlands, and be told, quite openly, it marked a private still.[41] He would not indeed make that journey, for there is now no Thurso coach. And even if he could, one little thing that happened to me could never happen to him, or not with the same trenchancy of contrast.

We had been upon the road all evening; the coach-top was crowded with Lews fishers going home, scarce anything but Gaelic had sounded in my ears; and our way had lain throughout over a moorish country very northern to behold. Latish at night, though it was still broad day in our subarctic latitude, we came down upon the shores of the roaring Pentland Firth,[42] that grave of mariners; on one hand, the cliffs of Dunnet Head ran seaward; in front was the little bare white town of Castleton, its streets full of blowing sand; nothing beyond, but the North Islands, the great deep, and the perennial ice-fields of the Pole. And here, in the last imaginable place, there sprang up young outlandish voices and a chatter of some foreign speech; and I saw, pursuing

38. Fishing village north of Wick.
39. Meg Merrilies is a gipsy woman in Scott's novel *Guy Mannering* (1815). Keats (1795–1821) wrote an eponymous poem about her on his 1818 trip to Scotland.
40. The stagecoach route that terminates in Thurso, a village on the north coast of Caithness.
41. An illegal whisky distillery.
42. The strait that separates the Orkney islands from Caithness on the mainland.

the coach with its load of Hebridean fishers—as they had pursued *vetturini*[43] up the passes of the Apennines or perhaps along the grotto under Virgil's tomb[44]—two little dark-eyed, white-toothed Italian vagabonds, of twelve to fourteen years of age, one with a hurdy-gurdy,[45] the other with a cage of white mice. The coach passed on, and their small Italian chatter died in the distance; and I was left to marvel how they had wandered into that country, and how they fared in it, and what they thought of it, and when (if ever) they should see again the silver wind-breaks run among the olives, and the stone-pine[46] stand guard upon Etruscan sepulchres.[47]

Upon any American, the strangeness of this incident is somewhat lost. For as far back as he goes in his own land, he will find some alien camping there; the Cornish miner, the French or Mexican half-blood, the negro in the South, these are deep in the woods and far among the mountains. But in an old, cold, and rugged country such as mine, the days of immigration are long at an end; and away up there, which was at that time far beyond the northernmost extreme of railways, hard upon the shore of that ill-omened strait of whirlpools, in a land of moors where no stranger came, unless it should be a sportsman to shoot grouse or an antiquary to decipher runes,[48] the presence of these small pedestrians struck the mind as though a bird-of-paradise had risen from the heather or an albatross come fishing in the bay of Wick. They were as

43. Coachmen.
44. In Naples.
45. The aforementioned stringed musical instrument with a hand crank.
46. A Mediterranean pine with an umbrella-like canopy.
47. An ancient civilization that flourished in central Italy from the eighth to the third century BC, the Etruscans built elaborate necropolises in towns and in the sides of hills.
48. Ancient Viking inscriptions.

strange to their surroundings as my lordly evangelist or the old Spanish grandee on the Fair Isle.[49]

49. Stevenson concludes "The Education of an Engineer" with an allusion to its companion piece, "The Coast of Fife," and to his account of two strangers who appeared out of nowhere on Fair Isle: a remote, windswept islet halfway between the Orkney archipelago and the largest of the Shetland Islands. In 1869, Stevenson encountered the first of the strangers himself: an "unshaven, poorly attired" "elderly gentleman," who carried a Greek Bible on the beach, and whom Stevenson later discovered was a lord. The second stranger made his appearance on Fair Isle three hundred years earlier: Alonso Pérez de Guzmán y de Zúñiga-Sotomayor, 7th Duke of Medina Sidonia and the Commander of the mighty Spanish Armada. The Duke was shipwrecked on Fair Isle in 1588, after being defeated by the English. With this image of a proud Spaniard stranded in the North Sea, Stevenson synthesizes the essay's Tower-of-Babel themes: the failed engineering project, the fall from grace, the inability to communicate, the scattering of tongues to the four corners of the earth. Stevenson's own failure as an engineer, however, marks the beginning of his education as a writer, for he must venture into the world to find his voice.

FRANÇOIS VILLON, STUDENT, POET AND HOUSEBREAKER

Perhaps one of the most curious revolutions in literary history is the sudden bull's-eye light[1] cast by M. Longnon[2] on the obscure existence of François Villon.[3] His book is not remarkable merely as a chapter of biography exhumed after four centuries.[4] To readers of the poet it will recall, with a flavour of satire, that characteristic passage in which he bequeaths his spectacles—with a humorous reservation of the case—to the hospital for blind paupers known as the Fifteen-Score.[5] Thus equipped, let the blind paupers go and separate the good from the bad in

1. A lantern with a planoconvex lens used as a flashlight by nightwatchmen and police officers.
2. Auguste Honoré Longnon (1844–1911), historian and author of *Biographical Study of François Villon, According to Unpublished Documents Held by the National Archives* (1877).
3. "Étude Biographique sur François Villon." Paris: H. Menu. [*Stevenson*]
4. Stevenson became obsessed with Villon after reading Longnon's book. The French poet-criminal repelled and attracted him in equal measure, and became a metaphor for radical freedom, as well as for the artist's marginalization in and damnation by society. That same year (1877), Stevenson wrote "A Lodging for the Night," a short story featuring Villon. In it, Stevenson confronts his fears of pursuing a literary career.
5. Villon's poem "Le Testament" (1461) takes the form of a last will and testament, in which he bequeaths various items to friends, strangers and enemies. His eyeglasses, minus the eyeglass case ("*Sans les estuys mes grans lunettes*"), he leaves to the residents of the Hospital of the Fifteen Score ("*je donne aux Quinze Vings*"), so-called because this Parisian home for the blind could accommodate three hundred residents.

the cemetery of the Innocents![6] For his own part the poet can see no distinction. Much have the dead people made of their advantages. What does it matter now that they have lain in state beds and nourished portly bodies upon cakes and cream! Here they all lie, to be trodden in the mud; the large estate and the small, sounding virtue and adroit or powerful vice, in very much the same condition; and a bishop not to be distinguished from a lamplighter with even the strongest spectacles.

Such was Villon's cynical philosophy. Four hundred years after his death, when surely all danger might be considered at an end, a pair of critical spectacles have been applied to his own remains; and though he left behind him a sufficiently ragged reputation from the first, it is only after these four hundred years that his delinquencies have been finally tracked home, and we can assign him to his proper place among the good or wicked. It is a staggering thought, and one that affords a fine figure of the imperishability of men's acts, that the stealth of the private inquiry office can be carried so far back into the dead and dusty past. We are not so soon quit of our concerns as Villon fancied. In the extreme of dissolution, when not so much as a man's name is remembered, when his dust is scattered to the four winds, and perhaps the very grave and the very graveyard where he was laid to rest have been forgotten, desecrated, and buried under populous towns,—even in this extreme let an antiquary fall across a sheet of manuscript, and the name will be recalled, the old infamy will pop out into daylight like a toad out of a fissure in the rock,[7] and the shadow of the shade of what was once a man will be heartily pilloried by his descendants. A little while ago and Villon was almost totally forgotten; then he was revived for the sake of his verses; and

6. The hospital was located in the Cemetery of the Innocents.

7. In the early nineteenth century, it was commonly believed that toads could live in perpetuity inside rocks. In 1828, for instance, geologist George Young claimed: "Instances of living toads, lodged within cavities in solid blocks of sandstone, have occurred in our district, as in many other places" (*A Geological Survey of the Yorkshire Coast*, p. 127).

now he is being revived with a vengeance in the detection of his misdemeanours. How unsubstantial is this projection of a man's existence, which can lie in abeyance for centuries and then be brushed up again and set forth for the consideration of posterity by a few dips in an antiquary's inkpot! This precarious tenure of fame goes a long way to justify those (and they are not few) who prefer cakes and cream in the immediate present.

A WILD YOUTH

François de Montcorbier, *alias* François des Loges, *alias* François Villon, *alias* Michel Mouton, Master of Arts in the University of Paris, was born in that city in the summer of 1431. It was a memorable year for France on other and higher considerations. A great-hearted girl and a poor-hearted boy made, the one her last, the other his first appearance on the public stage of that unhappy country.[8] On the 30th of May the ashes of Joan of Arc were thrown into the Seine, and on the 2nd of December our Henry Sixth made his Joyous Entry dismally enough into disaffected and depopulating Paris.[9] Sword and fire still ravaged the open country. On a single April Saturday twelve hundred persons, besides children, made their escape out of the starving capital. The hangman, as is not uninteresting to note in connection with Master Francis, was kept hard at work in 1431; on the last of April and on the 4th of May alone, sixty-two bandits swung from Paris gibbets.[10] A more confused or troublous time it would have been difficult to select for a start in life. Not even a man's nationality was certain; for the people of Paris there was no such thing as a Frenchman.

8. The "great-hearted girl" is nineteenth-year-old peasant Joan of Arc. Inspired by God, she led the French army against the English. After her capture, she was put on trial for heresy and witchcraft, and burned at the stake. The poor-hearted boy is Villon.
9. On December 16, 1431, ten-year-old King Henry VI of England was crowned King of France.
10. "Bourgeois de Paris," ed. Panthéon, pp. 688, 689. [*Stevenson*]

The English were the English indeed, but the French were only the Armagnacs,[11] whom, with Joan of Arc at their head, they had beaten back from under their ramparts not two years before. Such public sentiment as they had centred[12] about their dear Duke of Burgundy,[13] and the dear Duke had no more urgent business than to keep out of their neighbourhood. . . . At least, and whether he liked it or not, our disreputable troubadour was tubbed and swaddled as a subject of the English crown.

We hear nothing of Villon's father except that he was poor and of mean extraction. His mother was given piously, which does not imply very much in an old Frenchwoman, and quite uneducated. He had an uncle, a monk in an abbey at Angers,[14] who must have prospered beyond the family average, and was reported to be worth five or six hundred crowns. Of this uncle and his money-box the reader will hear once more. In 1448 Francis became a student of the University of Paris; in 1450 he took the degree of Bachelor, and in 1452 that of Master of Arts. His *bourse*, or the sum paid weekly for his board, was of the amount of two sous. Now two sous was about the price of a pound of salt butter in the bad times of 1417; it was the price of half-a-pound in the worse times of 1419; and in 1444, just four years before Villon joined the University, it seems to have been taken as the average wage for a day's manual labour.[15] In short, it cannot have been a very profuse allowance to keep a sharp-set lad in breakfast and supper for seven mortal days; and Villon's share of the cakes and pastry and general good

11. Embroiled in civil war, the France of 1431 consisted essentially of two nations controlled by three militaries. The House of Orléans, or the Armagnac faction, controlled central and southern France. The English controlled northern France (including Paris). England's allies, the House of Burgundy, ruled over southeast France and the Low Countries.
12. Formulated.
13. Philippe le Bon (1396–1467), Duke of Burgundy, had little connection to the people of Paris. His court moved between various palaces in modern-day Belgium.
14. Angers is a city 200 miles to the southwest of Paris.
15. "Bourgeois," pp. 627, 636, and 725. [*Stevenson*]

cheer, to which he is never weary of referring, must have been slender from the first.

The educational arrangements of the University of Paris were, to our way of thinking, somewhat incomplete. Worldly and monkish elements were presented in a curious confusion, which the youth might disentangle for himself. If he had an opportunity, on the one hand, of acquiring much hair-drawn divinity and a taste for formal disputation, he was put in the way of much gross and flaunting vice upon the other. The lecture room of a scholastic doctor was sometimes under the same roof with establishments of a very different and peculiarly unedifying order. The students had extraordinary privileges, which by all accounts they abused extraordinarily. And while some condemned themselves to an almost sepulchral regularity and seclusion, others fled the schools, swaggered in the street "with their thumbs in their girdle,"[16] passed the night in riot, and behaved themselves as the worthy forerunners of Jehan Frollo in the romance of "Notre Dame de Paris."[17] Villon tells us himself that he was among the truants, but we hardly needed his avowal. The burlesque erudition in which he sometimes indulged implies no more than the merest smattering of knowledge; whereas his acquaintance with blackguard haunts and industries could only have been acquired by early and consistent impiety and idleness. He passed his degrees, it is true; but some of us who have been to modern Universities will make their own reflections on the value of the test. As for his three pupils, Colin Laurent, Girard Gossouyn, and Jehan Marceau—if they were really his pupils in any serious sense—what can we say but God help them! And sure enough, by his own description, they

16. Seventeenth-century slang for "with an air of gravity or self-importance."
17. In *The Hunchback of Notre-Dame* (1831) by Victor Hugo (1802–1885), Jehan Frollo is a wayward student at the University of Paris. He is thrown to his death from one of the towers of Notre Dame Cathedral.

turned out as ragged, rowdy, and ignorant as was to be looked for from the views and manners of their rare preceptor.[18]

At some time or other, before or during his university career, the poet was adopted by Master Guillaume de Villon, chaplain of Saint Benoît-le-Bétourné, near the Sorbonne.[19] From him he borrowed the surname by which he is known to posterity. It was most likely from his house, called the "Porte Rouge,"[20] and situated in a garden in the cloister of St. Benoît, that Master Francis heard the bell of the Sorbonne ring out the Angelus[21] while he was finishing his "Small Testament"[22] at Christmastide in 1456. Towards this benefactor he usually gets credit for a respectable display of gratitude. But with his trap and pitfall style[23] of writing, it is easy to make too sure. His sentiments are about as much to be relied on as those of a professional beggar; and in this, as in so many other matters, he comes towards us whining and piping the eye, and goes off again with a whoop and his finger to his nose. Thus, he calls Guillaume de Villon his "more than father," thanks him with a great show of sincerity for having helped him out of many scrapes, and bequeaths him his portion of renown. But the portion of renown which belonged to a young thief, distinguished (if, at the period when he wrote this legacy, he was distinguished at all) for having written some more or less obscene and scurrilous ballads, must have been little fitted to gratify the self-respect or increase the reputation of a benevolent ecclesiastic. The same remark applies to a subsequent legacy of the poet's library, with specification of one work which was plainly neither decent nor

18. Tutor.
19. The Sorbonne was one of several colleges at the University of Paris. Its name later became synonymous with the University.
20. Red Door.
21. Catholic churches ring their bells at regular intervals throughout the day to remind the faithful to recite the Lord's Prayer, or the Angelus.
22. Villon's early poem "Le Lais" ("The Legacy") is sometimes called "The Small Testament" because it anticipates themes in "Le Testament," or "The Large Testament."
23. Facetious.

devout.[24] We are thus left on the horns of a dilemma. If the chaplain was a godly, philanthropic personage, who had tried to graft good principles and good behaviour on this wild slip of an adopted son, these jesting legacies would obviously cut him to the heart. The position of an adopted son towards his adoptive father is one full of delicacy; where a man lends his name he looks for great consideration. And this legacy of Villon's portion of renown may be taken as the mere fling of an unregenerate scapegrace who has wit enough to recognise in his own shame the readiest weapon of offence against a prosy benefactor's feelings. The gratitude of Master Francis figures, on this reading, as a frightful *minus* quantity. If, on the other hand, those jests were given and taken in good humour, the whole relation between the pair degenerates into the unedifying complicity of a debauched old chaplain and a witty and dissolute young scholar. At this rate the house with the red door may have rung with the most mundane minstrelsy; and it may have been below its roof that Villon, through a hole in the plaster, studied, as he tells us, the leisures of a rich ecclesiastic.[25]

It was, perhaps, of some moment in the poet's life that he should have inhabited the cloister of Saint Benoît. Three of the most remarkable among his early acquaintances are Catherine de Vausselles, for whom he entertained a short-lived affection and an enduring and most unmanly resentment; Regnier de Montigny, a young blackguard of good birth; and Colin de Cayeux, a fellow with a marked aptitude for picking locks. Now we are on a foundation of mere conjecture, but it is at least curious to find that two of the canons[26] of Saint Benoît answered respectively to the names of Pierre de Vaucel and Etienne de Montigny, and that

24. The work in question is "le Rommant du Pet au Deable" ("The Tale of the Devil's Fart").

25. In "The Testament," Villon recounts how he spied "through a hole in the mortise" ("*par ung trou de mortaise*") "a plump cleric" ("*ung gras chanoine*") lounging "naked" ("*nu*") with Lady Sidonia, with whom he was "laughing, toying, flirting and kissing" ("*Rire, jouer, mignonner et baisier*").

26. A clergyman belonging to the staff of a cathedral or collegiate church.

there was a householder called Nicolas de Cayeux in a street—the Rue des Poirées—in the immediate neighbourhood of the cloister. M. Longnon is almost ready to identify Catherine as the niece of Pierre; Regnier as the nephew of Etienne, and Colin as the son of Nicolas. Without going so far, it must be owned that the approximation of names is significant. As we go on to see the part played by each of these persons in the sordid melodrama of the poet's life, we shall come to regard it as even more notable. Is it not Clough who has remarked that, after all, everything lies in juxtaposition?[27] Many a man's destiny has been settled by nothing apparently more grave than a pretty face on the opposite side of the street and a couple of bad companions round the corner.

Catherine de Vausselles (or de Vaucel—the change is within the limits of Villon's licence) had plainly delighted in the poet's conversation; near neighbours or not, they were much together and Villon made no secret of his court, and suffered himself to believe that his feeling was repaid in kind. This may have been an error from the first, or he may have estranged her by subsequent misconduct or temerity. One can easily imagine Villon an impatient wooer. One thing, at least, is sure: that the affair terminated in a manner bitterly humiliating to Master Francis. In presence of his lady-love, perhaps under her window and certainly with her connivance, he was unmercifully thrashed by one Noë le Joly—beaten, as he says himself, like dirty linen on the washing-board.[28] It is characteristic that his malice had notably increased between the time when he wrote the "Small Testament" immediately on the back of the occurrence, and the time when he wrote the "Large

---

27. From *Amours de Voyage* (1849), a novel in verse by English poet Arthur Hugh Clough (1819–1861):

> Juxtaposition is great, but, you tell me, affinity greater.
> Ah, my friend, there are many affinities, greater and lesser,
> Stronger and weaker; and each, by the favour of juxtaposition,
> Potent, efficient, in force,—for a time (151–54)

28. *"J'en fus batu comme a ru tells."*

Testament" five years after. On the latter occasion nothing is too bad for his "damsel with the twisted nose,"[29] as he calls her. She is spared neither hint nor accusation, and he tells his messenger to accost her with the vilest insults.[30] Villon, it is thought, was out of Paris when these amenities escaped his pen; or perhaps the strong arm of Noë le Joly would have been again in requisition. So ends the love story, if love story it may properly be called. Poets are not necessarily fortunate in love; but they usually fall among more romantic circumstances and bear their disappointment with a better grace.

The neighbourhood[31] of Regnier de Montigny and Colin de Cayeux was probably more influential on his after life than the contempt of Catherine. For a man who is greedy of all pleasures, and provided with little money and less dignity of character, we may prophesy a safe and speedy voyage downward. Humble or even truckling[32] virtue may walk unspotted in this life. But only those who despise the pleasures can afford to despise the opinion of the world. A man of a strong, heady temperament, like Villon, is very differently tempted. His eyes lay hold on all provocations greedily, and his heart flames up at a look into imperious desire; he is snared and broached-to by anything and everything, from a pretty face to a piece of pastry in a cookshop window; he will drink the rinsing of the wine cup, stay the latest at the tavern party; tap at the lit windows, follow the sound of singing, and beat the whole neighbourhood for another reveller, as he goes reluctantly homeward; and grudge himself every hour of sleep as a black empty period in which he cannot follow after pleasure. Such a person is lost if he have not dignity, or, failing that, at least pride, which is its shadow and in many ways its substitute. Master Francis, I fancy, would follow his own eager instincts without much spiritual

29. *"Ma demoiselle au nez tortu."*
30. *"Orde paillarde"* ("Dirty whore").
31. Companionship.
32. Obsequious.

struggle. And we soon find him fallen among thieves in sober, literal earnest, and counting as acquaintances the most disreputable people he could lay his hands on: fellows who stole ducks in Paris Moat; sergeants of the criminal court, and archers of the watch; blackguards who slept at night under the butchers' stalls, and for whom the aforesaid archers peered about carefully with lanterns; Regnier de Montigny, Colin de Cayeux, and their crew, all bound on a favouring breeze towards the gallows; the disorderly abbess of Port Royal, who went about at fair-time with soldiers and thieves, and conducted her abbey on the queerest principles, and most likely Perette Mauger, the great Paris receiver of stolen goods, not yet dreaming, poor woman! of the last scene of her career when Henry Cousin, executor of the high justice, shall bury her, alive and most reluctant, in front of the new Montigny gibbet.[33] Nay, our friend soon began to take a foremost rank in this society. He could string off verses, which is always an agreeable talent; and he could make himself useful in many other ways. The whole ragged army of Bohemia, and whosoever loved good cheer without at all loving to work and pay for it, are addressed in contemporary verses as the "Subjects of François Villon." He was a good genius[34] to all hungry and unscrupulous persons; and became the hero of a whole legendary cycle of tavern tricks and cheateries. At best, these were doubtful levities, rather too thievish for a schoolboy, rather too gamesome for a thief. But he would not linger long in this equivocal border-land. He must soon have complied with his surroundings. He was one who would go where the cannikin[35] clinked, not caring who should pay; and from supping in the wolves' den, there is but a step to hunting with the pack. And here, as I am on the chapter of his degradation, I shall say all I mean to say about its darkest expression, and be done with it for good. Some charitable critics see no more than a *jeu*

33. "Chronique Scandaleuse," ed. Panthéon, p. 237. [*Stevenson*]
34. Attendant or tutelary spirit.
35. Drinking cup.

d'esprit,[36] a graceful and trifling exercise of the imagination, in the grimy ballad of Fat Peg (*Grosse Margot*).[37] I am not able to follow these gentlemen to this polite extreme. Out of all Villon's works that ballad stands forth in flaring reality, gross and ghastly, as a thing written in a contraction of disgust. M. Longnon shows us more and more clearly at every page that we are to read our poet literally, that his names are the names of real persons, and the events he chronicles were actual events. But even if the tendency of criticism had run the other way, this ballad would have gone far to prove itself. I can well understand the reluctance of worthy persons in this matter; for of course it is unpleasant to think of a man of genius as one who held, in the words of Marina to Boult—

> "A place, for which the pained'st fiend
> Of hell would not in reputation change."[38]

But beyond this natural unwillingness, the whole difficulty of the case springs from a highly virtuous ignorance of life. Paris now is not so different from the Paris of then; and the whole of the doings of Bohemia are not written in the sugar-candy pastorals of Mürger.[39] It is really not at all surprising that a young man of the fifteenth century, with a knack of making verses, should accept his bread upon disgraceful terms. The race of those who do so is not extinct; and some of them to this day write the prettiest verses imaginable. . . . After this, it were impossible for Master Francis to fall lower: to go and steal for himself would be an admirable advance from every point of view, divine or human.

36. Lighthearted or witty composition.

37. Perhaps Villon's bawdiest composition, the "Ballade de Grosse Margot" is a scatological account of Villon's sex life with his fat and flatulent girlfriend Margot. He brags of how he acted as her pimp, turned their home into a "brothel" ("*bordeau*"), and beat her when she didn't earn money.

38. From Shakespeare's *Pericles, Prince of Tyre* (4.6.168–69).

39. Henri Murger (1822–1861), French novelist and poet. Murger's romanticized account of life in the Latin Quarter of Paris, *Scènes de la vie de bohème* (1851), was the basis for Puccini's opera *La bohème* (1896).

And yet it is not as a thief, but as a homicide, that he makes his first appearance before angry justice. On June 5, 1455, when he was about twenty-four, and had been Master of Arts for a matter of three years, we behold him for the first time quite definitely. Angry justice had, as it were, photographed him in the act of his homicide; and M. Longnon, rummaging among old deeds, has turned up the negative and printed it off for our instruction. Villon had been supping—copiously we may believe—and sat on a stone bench in front of the Church of St. Benoît, in company with a priest called Gilles and a woman of the name of Isabeau. It was nine o'clock, a mighty late hour for the period, and evidently a fine summer's night. Master Francis carried a mantle, like a prudent man, to keep him from the dews (*serain*), and had a sword below it dangling from his girdle. So these three dallied in front of St Benoît, taking their pleasure (*pour soy esbatre*). Suddenly there arrived upon the scene a priest, Philippe Chermoye or Sermaise, also with sword and cloak, and accompanied by one Master Jehan le Mardi. Sermaise, according to Villon's account, which is all we have to go upon, came up blustering and denying God; as Villon rose to make room for him upon the bench, thrust him rudely back into his place; and finally drew his sword and cut open his lower lip, by what I should imagine was a very clumsy stroke. Up to this point, Villon professes to have been a model of courtesy, even of feebleness: and the brawl, in his version, reads like the fable of the wolf and the lamb. But now the lamb was roused; he drew his sword, stabbed Sermaise in the groin, knocked him on the head with a big stone, and then, leaving him to his fate, went away to have his own lip doctored by a barber of the name of Fouquet. In one version, he says that Gilles, Isabeau, and Le Mardi ran away at the first high words, and that he and Sermaise had it out alone; in another, Le Mardi is represented as returning and wresting Villon's sword from him: the reader may please himself. Sermaise was picked up, lay all that night in the prison of Saint Benoît, where he was examined by an official of the Châtelet[40] and expressly pardoned Villon, and died on the following Saturday in the Hôtel Dieu.[41]

This, as I have said, was in June. Not before January of the next year could Villon extract a pardon from the King; but while his hand was in, he got two. One is for "François des Loges, *alias* (*autrement dit*) de Villon"; and the other runs in the name of François de Montcorbier. Nay, it appears there was a further complication; for in the narrative of the first of these documents, it is mentioned that he passed himself off upon Fouquet, the barber-surgeon, as one Michel Mouton. M. Longnon has a theory that this unhappy accident with Sermaise was the cause of Villon's subsequent irregularities; and that up to that moment he had been the pink[42] of good behaviour. But the matter has to my eyes a more dubious air. A pardon necessary for Des Loges and another for Montcorbier? and these two the same person? and one or both of them known by the *alias* of Villon, however honestly come by? and lastly, in the heat of the moment, a fourth name thrown out with an assured countenance? A ship is not to be trusted that sails under so many colours. This is not the simple bearing of innocence. No—the young master was already treading crooked paths; already, he would start and blench at a hand upon his shoulder, with the look we know so well in the face of Hogarth's Idle Apprentice;[43] already, in the blue devils,[44] he would see Henry Cousin, the executor of high justice, going in dolorous procession towards Montfaucon,[45] and hear the wind and the birds crying around Paris gibbet.

40. A fortress that served as police headquarters.
41. A hospital in Paris.
42. Embodiment.
43. The etching *The Idle 'Prentice Executed at Tyburn* (1747) by William Hogarth (1697–1764) depicts a terror-stricken man being led in a cart to his execution. He is surrounded by hundreds of rowdy onlookers.
44. Delirium tremens.
45. The Gibbet of Montfaucon, where criminals were executed and their rotting corpses displayed, was located on a small hill outside the walls of Paris.

A GANG OF THIEVES

In spite of the prodigious number of people who managed to get hanged, the fifteenth century was by no means a bad time for criminals. A great confusion of parties and great dust of fighting favoured the escape of private housebreakers and quiet fellows who stole ducks in Paris Moat. Prisons were leaky; and as we shall see, a man with a few crowns in his pocket, and perhaps some acquaintance among the officials, could easily slip out and become once more a free marauder. There was no want of a sanctuary where he might harbour until troubles blew by; and accomplices helped each other with more or less good faith. Clerks,[46] above all, had remarkable facilities for a criminal way of life; for they were privileged, except in cases of notorious incorrigibility, to be plucked from the hands of rude secular justice and tried by a tribunal of their own. In 1402, a couple of thieves, both clerks of the University, were condemned to death by the Provost of Paris. As they were taken to Montfaucon, they kept crying "high and clearly" for their benefit of clergy, but were none the less pitilessly hanged and gibbeted. Indignant Alma Mater interfered before the King; and the Provost was deprived of all royal offices, and condemned to return the bodies and erect a great stone cross, on the road from Paris to the gibbet, graven with the effigies of these two holy martyrs.[47] We shall hear more of the benefit of clergy; for after this the reader will not be surprised to meet with thieves in the shape of tonsured clerks, or even priests and monks.

To a knot of such learned pilferers our poet certainly belonged; and by turning over a few more of M. Longnon's negatives, we shall get a clear idea of their character and doings. Montigny and

---

46. While they were not priests, students at the University of Paris were minor clerics. They were tonsured (their heads were shaved) and they received minor holy orders. Their clerical status meant that they were protected from the police, subject instead to ecclesiastical law.
47. Monstrelet: "Panthéon Littéraire," p. 26. [*Stevenson*]

De Cayeux are names already known; Guy Tabary, Petit-Jehan, Dom Nicolas, little Thibault, who was both clerk and goldsmith, and who made picklocks and melted plate for himself and his companions—with these the reader has still to become acquainted. Petit-Jehan and De Cayeux were handy fellows and enjoyed a useful pre-eminence in honour of their doings with the picklock. "*Dictus des Cahyeus est fortis operator crochetorum,*"[48] says Tabary's interrogation, "*sed dictus Petit-Jehan, ejus socius, est forcius operator.*"[49] But the flower of the flock was little Thibault; it was reported that no lock could stand before him; he had a persuasive hand; let us salute capacity wherever we may find it. Perhaps the term *gang* is not quite properly applied to the persons whose fortunes we are now about to follow; rather they were independent malefactors, socially intimate, and occasionally joining together for some serious operation just as modern stockjobbers[50] form a syndicate for an important loan. Nor were they at all particular to any branch of misdoing. They did not scrupulously confine themselves to a single sort of theft, as I hear is common among modern thieves. They were ready for anything, from pitch-and-toss[51] to manslaughter. Montigny, for instance, had neglected neither of these extremes, and we find him accused of cheating at games of hazard on the one hand, and on the other of the murder of one Thevenin Pensete in a house by the Cemetery of St. John. If time had only spared us some particulars, might not this last have furnished us with the matter of a grisly winter's tale?

At Christmas-time in 1456, readers of Villon will remember that he was engaged on the "Small Testament." About the same period, *circa festum nativitatis domini,*[52] he took part in a memorable supper at the Mule Tavern, in front of the Church of St. Mathurin.

48. "He said that De Cayeux is a skilled hand with lock picks."
49. "But he said that Petit-Jehan, his partner, is even more skilled."
50. Stockbrokers.
51. A gambling game played with coins.
52. "around Christmas"

Tabary, who seems to have been very much Villon's creature, had ordered the supper in the course of the afternoon. He was a man who had had troubles in his time and languished in the Bishop of Paris's prisons on a suspicion of picking locks; confiding, convivial, not very astute—who had copied out a whole improper romance with his own right hand. This supper-party was to be his first introduction to De Cayeux and Petit-Jehan, which was probably a matter of some concern to the poor man's muddy wits; in the sequel, at least, he speaks of both with an undisguised respect, based on professional inferiority in the matter of picklocks. Dom Nicolas, a Picardy monk, was the fifth and last at table. When supper had been despatched and fairly washed down, we may suppose, with white Baigneux or red Beaune, which were favourite wines among the fellowship, Tabary was solemnly sworn over to secrecy on the night's performances; and the party left the Mule and proceeded to an unoccupied house belonging to Robert de Saint-Simon. This, over a low wall, they entered without difficulty. All but Tabary took off their upper garments; a ladder was found and applied to the high wall which separated Saint-Simon's house from the court of the College of Navarre; the four fellows in their shirt-sleeves (as we might say) clambered over in a twinkling; and Master Guy Tabary remained alone beside the overcoats. From the court the burglars made their way into the vestry of the chapel, where they found a large chest, strengthened with iron bands and closed with four locks. One of these locks they picked, and then, by levering up the corner, forced the other three. Inside was a small coffer, of walnut wood, also barred with iron, but fastened with only three locks, which were all comfortably picked by way of the keyhole. In the walnut coffer—a joyous sight by our thieves' lantern—were five hundred crowns of gold. There was some talk of opening the aumries,[53] where, if they had only known, a booty eight or nine times greater lay ready to their hand; but one of

53. Cupboards or closets in a church.

the party (I have a humorous suspicion it was Dom Nicolas, the Picardy monk) hurried them away. It was ten o'clock when they mounted the ladder; it was about midnight before Tabary beheld them coming back. To him they gave ten crowns, and promised a share of a two-crown dinner on the morrow; whereat we may suppose his mouth watered. In course of time, he got wind of the real amount of their booty and understood how scurvily he had been used; but he seems to have borne no malice. How could he, against such superb operators as Petit-Jehan and De Cayeux; or a person like Villon, who could have made a new improper romance out of his own head, instead of merely copying an old one with mechanical right hand?

The rest of the winter was not uneventful for the gang. First they made a demonstration against the Church of St. Mathurin after chalices, and were ignominiously chased away by barking dogs. Then Tabary fell out with Casin Chollet, one of the fellows who stole ducks in Paris Moat, who subsequently became a sergeant of the Châtelet and distinguished himself by misconduct, followed by imprisonment and public castigation, during the wars of Louis Eleventh.[54] The quarrel was not conducted with a proper regard to the King's peace, and the pair publicly belaboured each other until the police stepped in, and Master Tabary was cast once more into the prisons of the Bishop. While he still lay in durance, another job was cleverly executed by the band in broad daylight, at the Augustine Monastery. Brother Guillaume Coiffier was beguiled by an accomplice to St. Mathurin to say mass; and during his absence, his chamber was entered and five or six hundred crowns in money and some silver plate successfully abstracted. A melancholy man was Coiffier on his return! Eight crowns from this adventure were forwarded by little Thibault to the incarcerated Tabary; and with these he bribed the jailor and reappeared in Paris taverns. Some time before or shortly after this, Villon set out for

54. King Louis XI (1423–1483) defeated the House of Burgundy and united France.

Angers, as he had promised in the "Small Testament." The object of this excursion was not merely to avoid the presence of his cruel mistress or the strong arm of Noë le Joly, but to plan a deliberate robbery on his uncle the monk. As soon as he had properly studied the ground, the others were to go over in force from Paris—picklocks and all—and away with my uncle's strongbox! This throws a comical sidelight on his own accusation against his relatives, that they had "forgotten natural duty" and disowned him because he was poor. A poor relation is a distasteful circumstance at the best, but a poor relation who plans deliberate robberies against those of his blood, and trudges hundreds of weary leagues to put them into execution, is surely a little on the wrong side of toleration. The uncle at Angers may have been monstrously undutiful; but the nephew from Paris was upsides with him.

On the 23rd April, that venerable and discreet person, Master Pierre Marchand, Curate and Prior of Paray-le-Monial, in the diocese of Chartres, arrived in Paris and put up at the sign of the Three Chandeliers, in the Rue de la Huchette. Next day, or the day after, as he was breakfasting at the sign of the Armchair, he fell into talk with two customers, one of whom was a priest and the other our friend Tabary. The idiotic Tabary became mighty confidential as to his past life. Pierre Marchand, who was an acquaintance of Guillaume Coiffier's and had sympathised with him over his loss, pricked up his ears at the mention of picklocks, and led on the transcriber of improper romances from one thing to another, until they were fast friends. For picklocks the Prior of Paray professed a keen curiosity; but Tabary, upon some late alarm, had thrown all his into the Seine. Let that be no difficulty, however, for was there not little Thibault, who could make them of all shapes and sizes, and to whom Tabary, smelling an accomplice, would be only too glad to introduce his new acquaintance? On the morrow, accordingly, they met; and Tabary, after having first wet his whistle at the Prior's expense, led him to Notre Dame and presented him to four or five "young companions," who were keeping sanctuary in the church. They were all clerks, recently escaped, like Tabary himself, from the episcopal prisons. Among these we may notice Thibault, the operator, a little fellow of twenty-six, wearing long hair behind. The Prior expressed, through Tabary, his anxiety to become their accomplice and altogether such as they were (*de leur sorte et de leurs complices*). Mighty polite they showed themselves, and made him many fine speeches in return. But for all that, perhaps because they had longer heads than Tabary, perhaps because it is less easy to wheedle men in a body, they kept obstinately to generalities and gave him no information as to their exploits, past, present, or to come. I suppose Tabary groaned under this reserve; for no sooner were he and the Prior out of the church than he fairly emptied his heart to him, gave him full details of many hanging matters in the past, and explained the future intentions of the band. The scheme of the hour was to rob another Augustine monk, Robert de la Porte, and in this the Prior agreed to take a hand with simulated greed. Thus, in the course of two days, he had turned this wineskin of a Tabary inside out. For a while longer the farce was carried on; the Prior was introduced to Petit-Jehan, whom he describes as a little, very smart man of thirty, with a black beard and a short jacket; an appointment was made and broken in the de la Porte affair; Tabary had some breakfast at the Prior's charge and leaked out more secrets under the influence of wine and friendship; and then all of a sudden, on the 17th of May, an alarm sprang up, the Prior picked up his skirts and walked quietly over to the Châtelet to make a deposition, and the whole band took to their heels and vanished out of Paris and the sight of the police.

Vanish as they like, they all go with a clog about their feet. Sooner or later, here or there, they will be caught in the fact, and ignominiously sent home. From our vantage of four centuries afterwards, it is odd and pitiful to watch the order in which the fugitives are captured and dragged in.

Montigny was the first. In August of that same year, he was laid by the heels on many grievous counts; sacrilegious robberies, frauds, incorrigibility, and that bad business about Thevenin Pensete in the house by the cemetery of St. John. He was reclaimed by the ecclesiastical authorities as a clerk; but the claim was rebutted on the score of incorrigibility, and ultimately fell to the ground; and he was condemned to death by the Provost of Paris. It was a very rude hour for Montigny, but hope was not yet over. He was a fellow of some birth; his father had been king's pantler;[55] his sister, probably married to someone about the Court, was in the family way,[56] and her health would be endangered if the execution was proceeded with. So down comes Charles the Seventh[57] with letters of mercy, commuting the penalty to a year in a dungeon on bread and water, and a pilgrimage to the shrine of St. James in Galicia.[58] Alas! the document was incomplete; it did not contain the full tale of Montigny's enormities; it did not recite that he had been denied benefit of clergy, and it said nothing about Thevenin Pensete. Montigny's hour was at hand. Benefit of clergy, honourable descent from king's pantler, sister in the family way, royal letters of commutation—all were of no avail. He had been in prison in Rouen, in Tours, in Bordeaux, and four times already in Paris; and out of all these he had come scatheless; but now he must make a little excursion as far as Montfaucon with Henry Cousin, executor of high justice. There let him swing among the carrion crows.

About a year later, in July 1458, the police laid hands on Tabary. Before the ecclesiastical commissary he was twice examined, and, on the latter occasion, put to the question ordinary and extraordinary.[59] What a dismal change from pleasant suppers at the Mule,

55. Servant who oversees the pantry.
56. Pregnant.
57. King of France.
58. The shrine is located in the Cathedral of Santiago de Compostela in Galicia in northwest Spain.
59. Tortured.

where he sat in triumph with expert operators and great wits! He is at the lees of life, poor rogue; and those fingers which once transcribed improper romances are now agonisingly stretched upon the rack. We have no sure knowledge, but we may have a shrewd guess of the conclusion. Tabary, the admirer, would go the same way as those whom he admired.

The last we hear of is Colin de Cayeux. He was caught in autumn 1460, in the great Church of St. Leu d'Esserens, which makes so fine a figure in the pleasant Oise valley between Creil and Beaumont. He was reclaimed by no less than two bishops; but the Procureur for the Provost held fast by incorrigible Colin. 1460 was an ill-starred year: for justice was making a clean sweep of "poor and indigent persons, thieves, cheats, and lockpickers," in the neighbourhood of Paris;[60] and Colin de Cayeux, with many others, was condemned to death and hanged.[61]

VILLON AND THE GALLOWS

Villon was still absent on the Angers expedition when the Prior of Paray sent such a bombshell among his accomplices; and the dates of his return and arrest remain undiscoverable. M. Campaux[62] plausibly enough opined for the autumn of 1457, which would make him closely follow on Montigny, and the first of those denounced by the Prior to fall into the toils. We may suppose, at least, that it was not long thereafter; we may suppose him competed for between lay and clerical Courts; and we may suppose him alternately pert and impudent, humble and fawning,

60. "Chron. Scand." *ut supra*. [*Stevenson*]

61. Here and there, principally in the order of events, this article differs from M. Longnon's own reading of his material. The ground on which he defers the execution of Montigny and De Cayeux beyond the date of their trials seems insufficient. There is a law of parsimony for the construction of historical documents; simplicity is the first duty of narration; and hanged they were. [*Stevenson*]

62. Antoine Campaux (1818–1901), author of *François Villon; His Life and His Works* (1859).

in his defence. But at the end of all supposing, we come upon some nuggets of fact. For first, he was put to the question by water.[63] He who had tossed off so many cups of white Baigneux or red Beaune, now drank water through linen folds, until his bowels were flooded and his heart stood still. After so much raising of the elbow, so much outcry of fictitious thirst, here at last was enough drinking for a lifetime. Truly, of our pleasant vices, the gods make whips to scourge us. And secondly he was condemned to be hanged. A man may have been expecting a catastrophe for years, and yet find himself unprepared when it arrives. Certainly, Villon found, in this legitimate issue of his career, a very staggering and grave consideration. Every beast, as he says, clings bitterly to a whole skin. If everything is lost, and even honour, life still remains; nay, and it becomes, like the ewe lamb in Nathan's parable,[64] as dear as all the rest. "Do you fancy," he asks, in a lively ballad, "that I had not enough philosophy under my hood to cry out: 'I appeal'? If I had made any bones about the matter, I should have been planted upright in the fields, by the St. Denis Road"—Montfaucon being on the way to St. Denis. An appeal to Parliament, as we saw in the case of Colin de Cayeux, did not necessarily lead to an acquittal or a commutation; and while the matter was pending, our poet had ample opportunity to reflect on his position. Hanging is a sharp argument, and to swing with many others on the gibbet adds a horrible corollary for the imagination. With the aspect of Montfaucon he was well acquainted; indeed, as the neighbourhood appears to have been sacred to junketing and nocturnal picnics of wild young men and women, he had probably studied it under all varieties of hour and weather. And now, as he lay in prison waiting the mortal push, these different aspects crowded back

63. Water torture; the forced ingestion of a large quantity of water.

64. When King David steals Bathsheba from her husband, the prophet Nathan reprimands him by telling him the story of the lamb. In the parable, a rich man with many flocks refuses, when asked, to sacrifice one of his sheep. Instead, he forces a poor man who has only one beloved lamb to sacrifice it. Nathan compares David to the rich man (II Samuel 12:1–8).

on his imagination with a new and startling significance; and he wrote a ballad, by way of epitaph for himself and his companions, which remains unique in the annals of mankind. It is, in the highest sense, a piece of his biography:—

> "La pluye nous a debuez et lavez,
> Et le soleil dessechez et noirciz;
> Pies, corbeaulx, nous ont les yeux cavez,
> Et arrachez la barbe et les sourcilz.
> Jamais, nul temps, nous ne sommes rassis;
> Puis çà, puis là, comme le vent varie,
> A son plaisir sans cesser nous charie,
> Plus becquetez d'oiseaulx que dez à couldre.
> Ne soyez donc de nostre confrairie,
> Mais priez Dieu que tous nous vueille absouldre."[65]

Here is some genuine thieves' literature after so much that was spurious; sharp as an etching, written with a shuddering soul. There is an intensity of consideration in the piece that shows it to be the transcript of familiar thoughts. It is the quintessence of many a doleful nightmare on the straw, when he felt himself swing helpless in the wind, and saw the birds turn about him, screaming and menacing his eyes.

And, after all, the Parliament changed his sentence into one of banishment; and to Roussillon, in Dauphiny, our poet

---

65.

> The rain has rinsed and washed us
> The sun dried us and turned us black
> Magpies and ravens have pecked out our eyes
> And plucked our beards and eyebrows
> Never ever can we stand still
> Now here, now there, as the wind shifts
> At its whim it keeps swinging us
> Pocked by birds worse than a sewing thimble
> Therefore don't join in our brotherhood
> But pray God that he absolve us all.
> (trans. Galway Kinnell)

must carry his woes without delay. Travellers between Lyons and Marseilles may remember a station on the line, some way below Vienne, where the Rhone fleets seaward between vine-clad hills. This was Villon's Siberia. It would be a little warm in summer perhaps, and a little cold in winter in that draughty valley between two great mountain fields; but what with the hills, and the racing river, and the fiery Rhone wines, he was little to be pitied on the conditions of his exile. Villon, in a remarkably bad ballad, written in a breath, heartily thanked and fulsomely belauded the Parliament; the *envoi*, like the proverbial post-script of a lady's letter, containing the pith of his performance in a request for three days' delay to settle his affairs and bid his friends farewell. He was probably not followed out of Paris, like Antoine Fradin, the popular preacher, another exile of a few years later, by weeping multitudes;[66] but I daresay one or two rogues of his acquaintance would keep him company for a mile or so on the south road, and drink a bottle with him before they turned. For banished people, in those days, seem to have set out on their own responsibility, in their own guard, and at their own expense. It was no joke to make one's way from Paris to Roussillon alone and penniless in the fifteenth century. Villon says he left a rag of his tails on every bush.[67] Indeed, he must have had many a weary tramp, many a slender meal, and many a to-do with blustering captains of the Ordonnance.[68] But with one of his light fingers, we may fancy that he took as good as he gave; for every rag of his tail, he would manage to indemnify himself upon the population in the shape of food, or wine, or ringing money; and his route would be traceable across France and Burgundy by housewives and innkeepers lamenting over petty thefts, like the track of a single human locust. A strange

66. "Chron. Scand.," p. 338. [*Stevenson*]
67. Villon claims in "Le Testament" that he was "chased like a slut" ("chassié fut comme ung souillon") from Paris to Roussillon, which is why scraps of his clothes were caught on so many bushes.
68. The King's army.

figure he must have cut in the eyes of the good country people: this ragged, blackguard city poet, with a smack of the Paris student, and a smack of the Paris street arab,[69] posting along the highways, in rain or sun, among the green fields and vineyards. For himself, he had no taste for rural loveliness; green fields and vineyards would be mighty indifferent to Master Francis; but he would often have his tongue in his cheek at the simplicity of rustic dupes, and often, at city gates, he might stop to contemplate the gibbet with its swinging bodies, and hug himself on his escape.

How long he stayed at Roussillon, how far he became the *protégé* of the Bourbons,[70] to whom that town belonged, or when it was that he took part, under the auspices of Charles of Orleans,[71] in a rhyming tournament to be referred to once again in the pages of the present volume, are matters that still remain in darkness, in spite of M. Longnon's diligent rummaging among archives. When we next find him, in summer 1461, alas! he is once more in durance: this time at Méun-sur-Loire, in the prisons of Thibault d'Aussigny, Bishop of Orleans. He had been lowered in a basket into a noisome pit, where he lay, all summer, gnawing hard crusts and railing upon fate. His teeth, he says, were like the teeth of a rake: a touch of haggard portraiture all the more real for being excessive and burlesque, and all the more proper to the man for being a caricature of his own misery. His eyes were "bandaged with thick walls." It might blow hurricanes overhead; the lightning might leap in high heaven; but no word of all this reached him in his noisome pit. "*Il n'entre, ou gist, n'escler ni tourbillon.*"[72] Above all, he was fevered with envy and anger at the freedom of others; and his heart flowed over into curses as he thought of Thibault d'Aussigny, walking the streets in God's sunlight, and blessing

69. Homeless child.
70. European royal house.
71. Charles, Duke of Orléans (1394–1465), poet and patron of the arts. Stevenson's *Familiar Studies of Men and Books* (1882) included an essay on Charles of Orléans, as well as this essay on Villon.
72. "He can't be reached, where he lies, by lightning or whirlwinds."

people with extended fingers. So much we find sharply lined in his own poems. Why he was cast again into prison—how he had again managed to shave the gallows—this we know not, nor, from the destruction of authorities,[73] are we ever likely to learn. But on October 2nd, 1461, or some day immediately preceding, the new King, Louis Eleventh, made his joyous entry into Méun. Now it was a part of the formality on such occasions for the new King to liberate certain prisoners; and so the basket was let down into Villon's pit, and hastily did Master Francis scramble in, and was most joyfully hauled up, and shot out, blinking and tottering, but once more a free man, into the blessed sun and wind. Now or never is the time for verses! Such a happy revolution would turn the head of a stocking-weaver, and set him jingling rhymes. And so—after a voyage to Paris, where he finds Montigny and De Cayeux clattering their bones upon the gibbet, and his three pupils roystering[74] in Paris streets, "with their thumbs under their girdles,"—down sits Master Francis to write his "Large Testament," and perpetuate his name in a sort of glorious ignominy.

THE "LARGE TESTAMENT"

Of this capital achievement and, with it, of Villon's style in general, it is here the place to speak. The "Large Testament" is a hurly-burly of cynical and sentimental reflections about life, jesting legacies to friends and enemies, and, interspersed among these, many admirable ballades, both serious and absurd. With so free a design, no thought that occurred to him would need to be dismissed without expression; and he could draw at full length the portrait of his own bedevilled soul, and of the bleak and blackguardly world which was the theatre of his exploits and sufferings. If the reader can conceive something between the slapdash inconsequence

73. Official documents.
74. Swaggering.

of Byron's "Don Juan"[75] and the racy humorous gravity and brief noble touches that distinguish the vernacular poems of Burns,[76] he will have formed some idea of Villon's style. To the latter writer—except in the ballades, which are quite his own, and can be paralleled from no other language known to me—he bears a particular resemblance. In common with Burns he has a certain rugged compression, a brutal vivacity of epithet, a homely vigour, a delight in local personalities, and an interest in many sides of life, that are often despised and passed over by more effete and cultured poets. Both also, in their strong, easy colloquial way, tend to become difficult and obscure; the obscurity in the case of Villon passing at times into the absolute darkness of cant language.[77] They are perhaps the only two great masters of expression who keep sending their readers to a glossary.

"Shall we not dare to say of a thief," asks Montaigne, "that he has a handsome leg?"[78] It is a far more serious claim that we have to put forward in behalf of Villon. Beside that of his contemporaries, his writing, so full of colour, so eloquent, so picturesque, stands out in an almost miraculous isolation. If only one or two of the chroniclers could have taken a leaf out of his book, history would have been a pastime, and the fifteenth century as present to our minds as the age of Charles Second.[79] This gallows-bird was the one great writer of his age and country, and initiated modern literature for France. Boileau,[80] long ago, in the period of perukes[81] and snuffboxes, recognised him as the first articulate poet in the language; and if we measure him, not by priority of merit, but living duration of influence, not on a comparison with obscure

75. Published between 1819 and 1824, the lengthy narrative poem *Don Juan* is Byron's mock-epic account of its hero's amorous adventures.
76. Robert Burns (1759–1796), Scottish Romantic poet.
77. Obscure slang.
78. From the essay "Of husbanding your will" by French philosopher Michel de Montaigne (1533–1592).
79. Charles II (1630–1685), King of England, Scotland and Ireland.
80. Nicolas Boileau-Despréaux (1636–1711), French poet and critic.
81. Wigs.

forerunners, but with great and famous successors, we shall instal this ragged and disreputable figure in a far higher niche in glory's temple than was ever dreamed of by the critic. It is, in itself, a memorable fact that, before 1542, in the very dawn of printing, and while modern France was in the making, the works of Villon ran through seven different editions. Out of him flows much of Rabelais;[82] and through Rabelais, directly and indirectly, a deep, permanent, and growing inspiration. Not only his style, but his callous pertinent way of looking upon the sordid and ugly sides of life, becomes every day a more specific feature in the literature of France. And only the other year, a work of some power appeared in Paris,[83] and appeared with infinite scandal, which owed its whole inner significance and much of its outward form to the study of our rhyming thief.

The world to which he introduces us is, as before said, blackguardly and bleak. Paris swarms before us, full of famine, shame, and death; monks and the servants of great lords hold high wassail upon cakes and pastry; the poor man licks his lips before the baker's window; people with patched eyes sprawl all night under the stalls; chuckling Tabary transcribes an improper romance; bare-bosomed lasses and ruffling students swagger in the streets; the drunkard goes stumbling homewards; the graveyard is full of bones; and away on Montfaucon, Colin de Cayeux and Montigny hang draggled in the rain. Is there nothing better to be seen than sordid misery and worthless joys? Only where the poor old mother of the poet kneels in church below painted windows, and makes tremulous supplication to the Mother of God.

82. François Rabelais (c.1490–1553), French monk, scholar and satirist.

83. Stevenson is referring to the scandal (and obscenity trial) that greeted the 1857 publication of *The Flowers of Evil* (*Les Fleurs du mal*) by poet Charles Baudelaire (1821–1867). Baudelaire's gritty account of illicit sex, death and criminality is thematically and stylistically inspired by Villon. While twenty years is not exactly "the other year," the scandal continued in fits and starts for another eleven years, as expanded editions of *Les Fleurs du mal* appeared in 1861 and (after Baudelaire's death) in 1868.

In our mixed world, full of green fields and happy lovers, where not long before, Joan of Arc had led one of the highest and noblest lives in the whole story of mankind, this was all worth chronicling that our poet could perceive. His eyes were indeed sealed with his own filth. He dwelt all his life in a pit more noisome than the dungeon at Méun. In the moral world, also, there are large phenomena not cognisable out of holes and corners. Loud winds blow, speeding home deep-laden ships and sweeping rubbish from the earth; the lightning leaps and cleans the face of heaven; high purposes and brave passions shake and sublimate men's spirits; and meanwhile, in the narrow dungeon of his soul, Villon is mumbling[84] crusts and picking vermin.

Along with this deadly gloom of outlook, we must take another characteristic of his work: its unrivalled insincerity. I can give no better similitude of this quality than I have given already: that he comes up with a whine, and runs away with a whoop and his finger to his nose. His pathos is that of a professional mendicant who should happen to be a man of genius; his levity that of a bitter street arab, full of bread. On a first reading, the pathetic passages preoccupy the reader, and he is cheated out of an alms in the shape of sympathy. But when the thing is studied the illusion fades away: in the transitions, above all, we can detect the evil, ironical temper of the man; and instead of a flighty work, where many crude but genuine feelings tumble together for the mastery as in the lists of tournament, we are tempted to think of the "Large Testament" as of one long-drawn epical grimace, pulled by a merry-andrew,[85] who has found a certain despicable eminence over human respect and human affections by perching himself astride upon the gallows. Between these two views, at best, all temperate judgments will be found to fall; and rather, as I imagine, towards the last.

84. Chewing ineffectively.
85. Clown.

There were two things on which he felt with perfect and, in one case, even threatening sincerity.

The first of these was an undisguised envy of those richer than himself. He was forever drawing a parallel, already exemplified from his own words, between the happy life of the well-to-do and the miseries of the poor. Burns, too proud and honest not to work, continued through all reverses to sing of poverty with a light, defiant note. Béranger[86] waited till he was himself beyond the reach of want, before writing the "Old Vagabond" or "Jacques." Samuel Johnson, although he was very sorry to be poor, "was a great arguer for the advantages of poverty" in his ill days.[87] Thus it is that brave men carry their crosses, and smile with the fox burrowing in their vitals. But Villon, who had not the courage to be poor with honesty, now whiningly implores our sympathy, now shows his teeth upon the dung-heap with an ugly snarl. He envies bitterly, envies passionately. Poverty, he protests, drives men to steal, as hunger makes the wolf sally from the forest. The poor, he goes on, will always have a carping word to say, or, if that outlet be denied, nourish rebellious thoughts. It is a calumny on the noble army of the poor. Thousands in a small way of life, ay, and even in the smallest, go through life with tenfold as much honour and dignity and peace of mind as the rich gluttons whose dainties and state-beds awakened Villon's covetous temper. And every morning's sun sees thousands who pass whistling to their toil. But Villon was the "*mauvais pauvre*" defined by Victor Hugo,[88] and, in its English expression, so admirably stereotyped by Dickens. He was the first wicked *sans-culotte*.[89] He is the man of genius with the moleskin

86. Pierre-Jean de Béranger (1780–1857), French poet and songwriter.
87. Quoted in Boswell's *The Life of Samuel Johnson* (See "An Apology for Idlers.").
88. Victor Hugo titled a chapter in *Les Misérables* (1862) "*Le mauvais pauvre*" ("The Noxious Poor"). While the title refers to a particular slum-dweller and his immediate family, the phrase "*mauvais pauvre*" has come to mean a type or class of people: those so pathologically poor that people recoil in horror.
89. Meaning "without breeches," the *sans-culottes* were the disgruntled lower-class people, laborers mainly, who comprised the anti-aristocratic mobs and

cap. He is mighty pathetic and beseeching here in the street, but I would not go down a dark road with him for a large consideration.

The second of the points on which he was genuine and emphatic was common to the middle ages; a deep and somewhat snivelling conviction of the transitory nature of this life and the pity and horror of death. Old age and the grave, with some dark and yet half-sceptical terror of an after-world—these were ideas that clung about his bones like a disease. An old ape, as he says, may play all the tricks in its repertory, and none of them will tickle an audience into good humour. "*Tousjours vieil synge est desplaisant.*"[90] It is not the old jester who receives most recognition at a tavern party, but the young fellow, fresh and handsome, who knows the new slang, and carries off his vice with a certain air. Of this, as a tavern jester himself, he would be pointedly conscious. As for the women with whom he was best acquainted, his reflections on their old age, in all their harrowing pathos, shall remain in the original for me. Horace has disgraced himself to something the same tune;[91] but what Horace throws out with an ill-favoured laugh, Villon dwells on with an almost maudlin whimper.

It is in death that he finds his truest inspiration; in the swift and sorrowful change that overtakes beauty; in the strange revolution by which great fortunes and renowns are diminished to a handful of churchyard dust; and in the utter passing away of what was once lovable and mighty. It is in this that the mixed texture of his thought enables him to reach such poignant and terrible effects, and to enhance pity with ridicule, like a man cutting capers to a funeral march. It is in this, also, that he rises out of himself into the higher spheres of art. So, in the ballade by which he is best known,[92] he rings the changes on names that once stood for

---

armies of the French Revolution (1789–99).

90. "An old monkey is always unpleasant."

91. In three notorious odes (1.25, 3.15 and 4.13), Horace (see "Æs Triplex") mocks the fading charms of Roman ladies Lydia, Chloris and Lyce, respectively.

92. "Ballade des dames du temps jadis" ("Ballad of the Ladies of Times Past").

beautiful and queenly women, and are now no more than letters and a legend. "Where are the snows of yester year?"[93] runs the burden. And so, in another not so famous,[94] he passes in review the different degrees of bygone men, from the holy Apostles and the golden Emperor of the East,[95] down to the heralds, pursuivants,[96] and trumpeters, who also bore their part in the world's pageantries and ate greedily at great folks' tables: all this to the refrain of "So much carry the winds away!"[97] Probably, there was some melancholy in his mind for a yet lower grade, and Montigny and Colin de Cayeux clattering their bones on Paris gibbet. Alas, and with so pitiful an experience of life, Villon can offer us nothing but terror and lamentation about death! No one has ever more skilfully communicated his own disenchantment; no one ever blown a more ear-piercing note of sadness. This unrepentant thief can attain neither to Christian confidence, nor to the spirit of the bright Greek saying, that whom the gods love die early. It is a poor heart, and a poorer age, that cannot accept the conditions of life with some heroic readiness.

* * * * * *

The date of the "Large Testament" is the last date in the poet's biography. After having achieved that admirable and despicable performance, he disappears into the night from whence he came. How or when he died, whether decently in bed or trussed up to a gallows, remains a riddle for foolhardy commentators. It appears his health had suffered in the pit at Méun; he was thirty years of age and quite bald; with the notch in his under lip where Sermaise had struck him with the sword, and what wrinkles the reader may

93. "*Mais ou sont les neiges d'antan?*"
94. "Ballade des seigneurs du temps jadis" ("Ballad of the Lords of Times Past").
95. Constantine the Great (c.AD 272 – AD 337), Roman emperor who moved the capitol from Rome to Byzantium (modern-day Istanbul).
96. Attendants.
97. "*Autant en emporte ly vens.*"

imagine. In default of portraits, that is all I have been able to piece together, and perhaps even the baldness should be taken as a figure[98] of his destitution. A sinister dog, in all likelihood, but with a look in his eye, and the loose flexile mouth that goes with wit and an overweening sensual temperament. Certainly the sorriest figure on the rolls of fame.

98. Metaphor for.

CRABBED AGE AND YOUTH

"You know my mother now and then argues very notably; always very warmly at least. I happen often to differ from her; and we both think so well of our own arguments, that we very seldom are so happy as to convince one another. A pretty common case, I believe, in all *vehement* debatings. She says, I am *too witty;* Anglicé,[1] *too pert;* I, that she is *too wise;* that is to say, being likewise put into English, *not so young as she has been.*"—MISS HOWE to MISS HARLOWE, "Clarissa," vol. ii. Letter xiii.[2]

There is a strong feeling in favour of cowardly and prudential proverbs. The sentiments of a man while he is full of ardour and hope are to be received, it is supposed, with some qualification. But when the same person has ignominiously failed and begins to eat up his words, he should be listened to like an oracle. Most of our pocket wisdom is conceived for the use of mediocre people, to discourage them from ambitious attempts,

1. As the English would say.
2. *Clarissa: Or the History of a Young Lady* (1748), an epistolary novel by Samuel Richardson (1689–1761).

and generally console them in their mediocrity. And since mediocre people constitute the bulk of humanity, this is no doubt very properly so. But it does not follow that the one sort of proposition is any less true than the other, or that Icarus[3] is not to be more praised, and perhaps more envied, than Mr. Samuel Budgett, the Successful Merchant. The one is dead, to be sure, while the other is still in his counting-house counting out his money; and doubtless this is a consideration. But we have, on the other hand, some bold and magnanimous sayings common to high races and natures, which set forth the advantage of the losing side, and proclaim it better to be a dead lion than a living dog. It is difficult to fancy how the mediocrities reconcile such sayings with their proverbs. According to the latter, every lad who goes to sea is an egregious ass; never to forget your umbrella through a long life would seem a higher and wiser flight of achievement than to go smiling to the stake; and so long as you are a bit of a coward and inflexible in money matters, you fulfil the whole duty of man.

It is a still more difficult consideration for our average men, that while all their teachers, from Solomon down to Benjamin Franklin and the ungodly Binney,[4] have inculcated the same ideal of manners, caution, and respectability, those characters in history who have most notoriously flown in the face of such precepts are spoken of in hyperbolical terms of praise, and honoured with public monuments in the streets of our commercial centres. This is very bewildering to the moral sense. You have Joan of Arc, who left a humble but honest and reputable livelihood under the eyes of her parents, to go a-colonelling, in the company of rowdy soldiers, against the enemies of France; surely a melancholy example for one's daughters! And then you have Columbus, who

3. In Greek mythology, Icarus is the boy who flew too close to the sun. To escape from Crete, his engineer father, Daedalus, constructed enormous wings from feathers and wax. Ignoring his father's warnings, Icarus soared into the stratosphere. The wax melted, and he plummeted to his death.

4. Thomas Binney (1798–1874), Nonconformist minister who wrote advice books for young men.

may have pioneered America, but when all is said, was a most imprudent navigator. His Life is not the kind of thing one would like to put into the hands of young people; rather, one would do one's utmost to keep it from their knowledge, as a red flag of adventure and disintegrating influence in life. The time would fail me if I were to recite all the big names in history whose exploits are perfectly irrational and even shocking to the business mind. The incongruity is speaking;[5] and I imagine it must engender among the mediocrities a very peculiar attitude towards the nobler and showier sides of national life. They will read of the Charge of Balaclava[6] in much the same spirit as they assist at a performance of the *Lyons Mail*.[7] Persons of substance take in the *Times* and sit composedly in pit or boxes according to the degree of their prosperity in business. As for the generals who go galloping up and down among bomb-shells in absurd cocked hats—as for the actors who raddle[8] their faces and demean themselves for hire upon the stage—they must belong, thank God! to a different order of beings, whom we watch as we watch the clouds careering in the windy, bottomless inane, or read about like characters in ancient and rather fabulous annals. Our offspring would no more think of copying their behaviour, let us hope, than of doffing their clothes and painting themselves blue in consequence of certain admissions in the first chapter of their school history of England.[9]

Discredited as they are in practice, the cowardly proverbs hold their own in theory; and it is another instance of the same spirit,

---

5. Obvious.
6. The ill-fated charge of the British light cavalry against Russian artillerymen in the Crimean War (See "Æs Triplex.").
7. *The Lyons Mail* is an English-language adaptation of the French melodrama *Le Courrier de Lyons* (1850) by Paul Siraudin (1812–1883) and Eugène Moreau (1806–1876). The great Henry Irving (1838–1905) starred in a revival of the play months before Stevenson wrote "Crabbed Age and Youth."
8. Paint with rouge.
9. The Picts—an Iron Age people who inhabited northeastern Scotland into the early medieval period—were called the "painted people," because they tattooed their bodies and wore blue war paint.

that the opinions of old men about life have been accepted as final. All sorts of allowances are made for the illusions of youth; and none, or almost none, for the disenchantments of age. It is held to be a good taunt, and somehow or other to clinch the question logically, when an old gentleman waggles his head and says: "Ah, so I thought when I was your age." It is not thought an answer at all, if the young man retorts: "My venerable sir, so I shall most probably think when I am yours." And yet the one is as good as the other: pass for pass, tit for tat, a Roland for an Oliver.[10]

"Opinion in good men," says Milton, "is but knowledge in the making."[11] All opinions, properly so called, are stages on the road to truth. It does not follow that a man will travel any further; but if he has really considered the world and drawn a conclusion, he has travelled as far. This does not apply to formulae got by rote, which are stages on the road to nowhere but second childhood and the grave. To have a catchword in your mouth is not the same thing as to hold an opinion; still less is it the same thing as to have made one for yourself. There are too many of these catchwords in the world for people to rap out upon you like an oath and by way of an argument. They have a currency as intellectual counters; and many respectable persons pay their way with nothing else. They seem to stand for vague bodies of theory in the background. The imputed virtue of folios full of knockdown arguments is supposed to reside in them, just as some of the majesty of the British Empire dwells in the constable's truncheon. They are used in pure superstition, as old clodhoppers spoil Latin by way of an exorcism. And yet they are vastly serviceable for checking unprofitable discussion and stopping the mouths of babes and sucklings. And when a young man comes to a certain stage of intellectual growth, the examination of these counters forms a gymnastic at once amusing and fortifying to the mind.

10. A British expression meaning "an adequate response."
11. From *Areopagitica* (1644) by John Milton (1608–1674).

Because I have reached Paris, I am not ashamed of having passed through Newhaven and Dieppe.[12] They were very good places to pass through, and I am none the less at my destination. All my old opinions were only stages on the way to the one I now hold, as itself is only a stage on the way to something else. I am no more abashed at having been a red-hot Socialist with a panacea of my own than at having been a sucking infant. Doubtless the world is quite right in a million ways; but you have to be kicked about a little to convince you of the fact. And in the meanwhile you must do something, be something, believe something. It is not possible to keep the mind in a state of accurate balance and blank; and even if you could do so, instead of coming ultimately to the right conclusion, you would be very apt to remain in a state of balance and blank to perpetuity. Even in quite intermediate stages, a dash of enthusiasm is not a thing to be ashamed of in the retrospect: if St. Paul had not been a very zealous Pharisee, he would have been a colder Christian. For my part, I look back to the time when I was a Socialist with something like regret. I have convinced myself (for the moment) that we had better leave these great changes to what we call great blind forces; their blindness being so much more perspicacious than the little, peering, partial eyesight of men. I seem to see that my own scheme would not answer; and all the other schemes I ever heard propounded would depress some elements of goodness just as much as they encouraged others. Now I know that in thus turning Conservative with years, I am going through the normal cycle of change and travelling in the common orbit of men's opinions. I submit to this, as I would submit to gout or grey hair, as a concomitant of growing age or else of failing animal heat; but I do not acknowledge that it is necessarily a change for the better—I dare say it is deplorably for the worse. I have no choice in the business, and can no more resist this tendency of my mind than I could prevent my body from

12. Port towns and ferry terminals in England and France, respectively.

beginning to totter and decay. If I am spared (as the phrase runs) I shall doubtless outlive some troublesome desires; but I am in no hurry about that; nor, when the time comes, shall I plume myself on the immunity. Just in the same way, I do not greatly pride myself on having outlived my belief in the fairy tales of Socialism. Old people have faults of their own; they tend to become cowardly, niggardly, and suspicious. Whether from the growth of experience or the decline of animal heat, I see that age leads to these and certain other faults; and it follows, of course, that while in one sense I hope I am journeying towards the truth, in another I am indubitably posting towards these forms and sources of error.

As we go catching and catching at this or that corner of knowledge, now getting a foresight of generous possibilities, now chilled with a glimpse of prudence, we may compare the headlong course of our years to a swift torrent in which a man is carried away; now he is dashed against a boulder, now he grapples for a moment to a trailing spray;[13] at the end, he is hurled out and overwhelmed in a dark and bottomless ocean. We have no more than glimpses and touches; we are torn away from our theories; we are spun round and round and shown this or the other view of life, until only fools or knaves can hold to their opinions. We take a sight at a condition in life, and say we have studied it; our most elaborate view is no more than an impression. If we had breathing space, we should take the occasion to modify and adjust; but at this breakneck hurry, we are no sooner boys than we are adult, no sooner in love than married or jilted, no sooner one age than we begin to be another, and no sooner in the fulness of our manhood than we begin to decline towards the grave. It is in vain to seek for consistency or expect clear and stable views in a medium so perturbed and fleeting. This is no cabinet[14] science, in which things are tested to a scruple; we theorize with a pistol to our head; we

13. Branch.
14. Laboratory.

are confronted with a new set of conditions on which we have not only to pass a judgment, but to take action, before the hour is at an end. And we cannot even regard ourselves as a constant; in this flux of things, our identity itself seems in a perpetual variation; and not infrequently we find our own disguise the strangest in the masquerade. In the course of time, we grow to love things we hated and hate things we loved. Milton is not so dull as he once was, nor perhaps Ainsworth[15] so amusing. It is decidedly harder to climb trees, and not nearly so hard to sit still. There is no use pretending; even the thrice royal game of hide and seek has somehow lost in zest. All our attributes are modified or changed; and it will be a poor account of us if our views do not modify and change in a proportion. To hold the same views at forty as we held at twenty is to have been stupefied for a score of years, and take rank, not as a prophet, but as an unteachable brat, well birched,[16] and none the wiser. It is as if a ship captain should sail to India from the Port of London; and having brought a chart of the Thames on deck at his first setting out, should obstinately use no other for the whole voyage.

And mark you, it would be no less foolish to begin at Gravesend[17] with a chart of the Red Sea. *Si Jeunesse savait, si Vieillesse pouvait,*[18] is a very pretty sentiment, but not necessarily right. In five cases out of ten, it is not so much that the young people do not know, as that they do not choose. There is something irreverent in the speculation, but perhaps the want of power has more to do with the wise resolutions of age than we are always willing to admit. It would be an instructive experiment to make an old man young again and leave him all his *savoir.*[19] I scarcely think he would put his money in the Savings Bank after all; I doubt if he

15. William Harrison Ainsworth (1805–1882), British novelist known for his lurid tales of criminal adventure.
16. Whipped with the schoolmaster's rod.
17. A town in Kent near the mouth of the Thames.
18. If youth only knew, if age only could!
19. Knowing.

would be such an admirable son as we are led to expect; and as for his conduct in love, I believe firmly he would out-Herod Herod,[20] and put the whole of his new compeers[21] to the blush. Prudence is a wooden Juggernaut,[22] before whom Benjamin Franklin walks with the portly air of a high priest, and after whom dances many a successful merchant in the character of Atys.[23] But it is not a deity to cultivate in youth. If a man lives to any considerable age, it cannot be denied that he laments his imprudencies, but I notice he often laments his youth a deal more bitterly and with a more genuine intonation.

It is customary to say that age should be considered, because it comes last. It seems just as much to the point, that youth comes first. And the scale fairly kicks the beam, if you go on to add that age, in a majority of cases, never comes at all. Disease and accident make short work of even the most prosperous persons; death costs nothing, and the expense of a headstone is an inconsiderable trifle to the happy heir. To be suddenly snuffed out in the middle of ambitious schemes is tragical enough at best; but when a man has been grudging himself his own life in the meanwhile, and saving up everything for the festival that was never to be, it becomes that hysterically moving sort of tragedy which lies on the confines of farce. The victim is dead—and he has cunningly overreached himself: a combination of calamities none the less absurd for being grim. To husband a favourite claret until the batch turns sour, is not at all an artful stroke of policy; and how much more with a whole cellar—a whole bodily existence! People may lay down their lives with cheerfulness in the sure expectation of a blessed immortality; but that is a different affair from giving up youth with all its admirable pleasures, in the hope of a better

20. King Herod had nine concubines.
21. Companions.
22. A sacred wagon bearing the image of a Hindu god.
23. In Greek mythology, Attis was god of vegetation and consort to the goddess Cybele. In a fit of madness, he castrated himself.

quality of gruel in a more than problematical, nay, more than improbable, old age. We should not compliment a hungry man, who should refuse a whole dinner and reserve all his appetite for the dessert, before he knew whether there was to be any dessert or not. If there be such a thing as imprudence in the world, we surely have it here. We sail in leaky bottoms and on great and perilous waters; and to take a cue from the dolorous old naval ballad, we have heard the mermaids singing,[24] and know that we shall never see dry land any more. Old and young, we are all on our last cruise. If there is a fill of tobacco among the crew, for God's sake pass it round, and let us have a pipe before we go!

Indeed, by the report of our elders, this nervous preparation for old age is only trouble thrown away. We fall on guard, and after all it is a friend who comes to meet us. After the sun is down and the west faded, the heavens begin to fill with shining stars. So, as we grow old, a sort of equable jog-trot of feeling is substituted for the violent ups and downs of passion and disgust; the same influence that restrains our hopes, quiets our apprehensions; if the pleasures are less intense, the troubles are milder and more tolerable; and in a word, this period for which we are asked to hoard up everything as for a time of famine, is, in its own right, the richest, easiest, and happiest of life.

Nay, by managing its own work and following its own happy inspiration, youth is doing the best it can to endow the leisure of age. A full, busy youth is your only prelude to a self-contained and independent age; and the muff[25] inevitably develops into the bore. There are not many Doctor Johnsons,[26] to set forth upon their first romantic voyage at sixty-four. If we wish to scale Mont Blanc or visit a thieves' kitchen[27] in the East End, to go down

24. In seventeenth- and eighteenth-century English sea ballads, mermaids often appear as harbingers of disaster.
25. Bumbler.
26. Samuel Johnson (See "Æs Triplex.").
27. A slum.

in a diving-dress or up in a balloon, we must be about it while we are still young. It will not do to delay until we are clogged with prudence and limping with rheumatism, and people begin to ask us: "What does Gravity out of bed?" Youth is the time to go flashing from one end of the world to the other both in mind and body; to try the manners of different nations; to hear the chimes at midnight; to see sunrise in town and country; to be converted at a revival; to circumnavigate the metaphysics, write halting verses, run a mile to see a fire, and wait all day long in the theatre to applaud *Hernani*.[28] There is some meaning in the old theory about wild oats; and a man who has not had his green-sickness[29] and got done with it for good, is as little to be depended on as an unvaccinated infant. "It is extraordinary," says Lord Beaconsfield,[30] one of the brightest and best preserved of youths up to the date of his last novel,[31] "it is extraordinary how hourly and how violently change the feelings of an inexperienced young man." And this mobility is a special talent entrusted to his care; a sort of indestructible virginity; a magic armour, with which he can pass unhurt through great dangers and come unbedaubed out of the miriest passages. Let him voyage, speculate, see all that he can, do all that he may; his soul has as many lives as a cat; he will live in all weathers, and never be a halfpenny the worse. Those who go to the devil in youth, with anything like a fair chance, were probably little worth saving from the first; they must have been feeble fellows—creatures made of putty and packthread, without steel or fire, anger or true joyfulness, in their composition; we may

28. *Ernani* (1844), an opera by Giuseppe Verdi (1813–1901).
29. "The disease of virgins." The green is a reference to the jaundiced appearance of anemic girls, which was attributed in the popular imagination to lovesickness. In Shakespeare's *Romeo and Juliet* (1597), an enraged Capulet says to his daughter: "Out, you greensickness carrion! Out, you baggage! / You tallow-face!" (3.5.157–58).
30. From *The Young Duke* (1831) by Benjamin Disraeli, Earl of Beaconsfield (1804–1881), Prime Minister, novelist and historian. Disraeli was seventy-four when Stevenson wrote "Crabbed Age and Youth."
31. "Lothair." [*Stevenson*]

sympathize with their parents, but there is not much cause to go into mourning for themselves; for, to be quite honest, the weak brother is the worst of mankind.

When the old man waggles his head and says, "Ah, so I thought when I was your age," he has proved the youth's case. Doubtless, whether from growth of experience or decline of animal heat, he thinks so no longer; but he thought so while he was young; and all men have thought so while they were young, since there was dew in the morning or hawthorn in May; and here is another young man adding his vote to those of previous generations and rivetting another link to the chain of testimony. It is as natural and as right for a young man to be imprudent and exaggerated, to live in swoops and circles, and beat about his cage like any other wild thing newly captured, as it is for old men to turn grey, or mothers to love their offspring, or heroes to die for something worthier than their lives.

By way of an apologue[32] for the aged, when they feel more than usually tempted to offer their advice, let me recommend the following little tale. A child who had been remarkably fond of toys (and in particular of lead soldiers) found himself growing to the level of acknowledged boyhood without any abatement of this childish taste. He was thirteen; already he had been taunted for dallying over-long about the playbox; he had to blush if he was found among his lead soldiers; the shades of the prison-house were closing about him with a vengeance. There is nothing more difficult than to put the thoughts of children into the language of their elders; but this is the effect of his meditations at this juncture: "Plainly," he said, "I must give up my playthings in the meanwhile, since I am not in a position to secure myself against idle jeers. At the same time, I am sure that playthings are the very pick of life; all people give them up out of the same pusillanimous respect for those who are a little older; and if they do not return to them as

32. Moral fable.

soon as they can, it is only because they grow stupid and forget. I shall be wiser; I shall conform for a little to the ways of their foolish world; but so soon as I have made enough money, I shall retire and shut myself up among my playthings until the day I die." Nay, as he was passing in the train along the Esterel mountains[33] between Cannes and Fréjus, he remarked a pretty house in an orange garden at the angle of a bay, and decided that this should be his Happy Valley.[34] Astraea Redux;[35] childhood was to come again! The idea has an air of simple nobility to me, not unworthy of Cincinnatus.[36] And yet, as the reader has probably anticipated, it is never likely to be carried into effect. There was a worm i' the bud, a fatal error in the premises. Childhood must pass away, and then youth, as surely as age approaches. The true wisdom is to be always seasonable, and to change with a good grace in changing circumstances. To love playthings well as a child, to lead an adventurous and honourable youth, and to settle when the time arrives, into a green and smiling age, is to be a good artist in life and deserve well of yourself and your neighbour.

You need repent none of your youthful vagaries. They may have been over the score on one side, just as those of age are probably over the score on the other. But they had a point; they not only befitted your age and expressed its attitude and passions, but they had a relation to what was outside of you, and implied criticisms on the existing state of things, which you need not allow to have been undeserved, because you now see that they were partial. All error, not merely verbal, is a strong way of stating that

33. A coastal mountain range in southeast France.

34. In Samuel Johnson's novella *The History of Rasselas, Prince of Abissinia* (1759), Happy Valley is the idyllic setting of the royal palace, where the young prince lives until he comes of age. The expression "Happy Valley" means a place of unparalleled beauty and tranquility.

35. Justice Restored. Stevenson borrows this Latin phrase from John Dryden (1631–1700), whose poem "Astraea Redux" (1660) celebrates the restoration of the monarchy in England.

36. Lucius Quinctius Cincinnatus (c.519–430 BC), Roman statesman and symbol of civic virtue.

the current truth is incomplete. The follies of youth have a basis in sound reason, just as much as the embarrassing questions put by babes and sucklings. Their most anti-social acts indicate the defects of our society. When the torrent sweeps the man against a boulder, you must expect him to scream, and you need not be surprised if the scream is sometimes a theory. Shelley,[37] chafing at the Church of England, discovered the cure of all evils in universal atheism. Generous lads irritated at the injustices of society see nothing for it but the abolishment of everything and Kingdom Come of anarchy. Shelley was a young fool; so are these cock-sparrow[38] revolutionaries. But it is better to be a fool than to be dead. It is better to emit a scream in the shape of a theory than to be entirely insensible to the jars and incongruities of life and take everything as it comes in a forlorn stupidity. Some people swallow the universe like a pill; they travel on through the world, like smiling images pushed from behind. For God's sake give me the young man who has brains enough to make a fool of himself! As for the others, the irony of facts shall take it out of their hands, and make fools of them in downright earnest, ere the farce be over. There shall be such a mopping and a mowing at the last day, and such blushing and confusion of countenance for all those who have been wise in their own esteem, and have not learnt the rough lessons that youth hands on to age. If we are indeed here to perfect and complete our own natures, and grow larger, stronger, and more sympathetic against some nobler career in the future, we had all best bestir ourselves to the utmost while we have the time. To equip a dull, respectable person with wings would be but to make a parody of an angel.

In short, if youth is not quite right in its opinions, there is a strong probability that age is not much more so. Undying hope is co-ruler of the human bosom with infallible credulity. A man finds

37. Percy Bysshe Shelley (1792–1822), Romantic poet.
38. Cocky and quarrelsome.

he has been wrong at every preceding stage of his career, only to deduce the astonishing conclusion that he is at last entirely right. Mankind, after centuries of failure, are still upon the eve of a thoroughly constitutional millennium. Since we have explored the maze so long without result, it follows, for poor human reason, that we cannot have to explore much longer; close by must be the centre, with a champagne luncheon and a piece of ornamental water.[39] How if there were no centre at all, but just one alley after another, and the whole world a labyrinth without end or issue?

I overheard the other day a scrap of conversation, which I take the liberty to reproduce. "What I advance is true," said one. "But not the whole truth," answered the other. "Sir," returned the first (and it seemed to me there was a smack of Dr. Johnson in the speech), "Sir, there is no such thing as the whole truth!" Indeed, there is nothing so evident in life as that there are two sides to a question. History is one long illustration. The forces of nature are engaged, day by day, in cudgelling it into our backward intelligences. We never pause for a moment's consideration, but we admit it as an axiom. An enthusiast sways humanity exactly by disregarding this great truth, and dinning it into our ears that this or that question has only one possible solution; and your enthusiast is a fine florid fellow, dominates things for a while and shakes the world out of a doze; but when once he is gone, an army of quiet and uninfluential people set to work to remind us of the other side and demolish the generous imposture. While Calvin[40] is putting everybody exactly right in his "Institutes," and hot-headed Knox[41] is thundering in the pulpit, Montaigne[42] is already looking at the other side in his library in Périgord, and predicting that they will find as much to quarrel about in the Bible

39. Ornamental pond or water garden.
40. John Calvin (1509–1564), French theologian, leader of the Protestant Reformation, and author of *Institutes of the Christian Religion* (1536).
41. John Knox (c.1513–1572), theologian and founder of the Presbyterian Church of Scotland.
42. Michel de Montaigne (1533–1592), philosopher and essayist.

as they had found already in the Church. Age may have one side, but assuredly Youth has the other. There is nothing more certain than that both are right, except perhaps that both are wrong. Let them agree to differ; for who knows but what agreeing to differ may not be a form of agreement rather than a form of difference?

I suppose it is written that anyone who sets up for a bit of a philosopher must contradict himself to his very face. For here have I fairly talked myself into thinking that we have the whole thing before us at last; that there is no answer to the mystery, except that there are as many as you please; that there is no centre to the maze because, like the famous sphere, its centre is everywhere;[43] and that agreeing to differ with every ceremony of politeness, is the only "one undisturbed song of pure concent"[44] to which we are ever likely to lend our musical voices.

43. From the twelfth-century *Book of the Twenty-Four Philosophers*: "God is an infinite sphere whose center is everywhere and whose circumference is nowhere" (*Deus est sphaera infinita, cuius centrum est ubique, circumferentia nusquam*). Five hundred years later, in his *Pensées* (1669), Blaise Pascal (1623–1662), French mathematician, reworked the famous phrase, substituting "Nature" for "God."

44. From Milton's "At a Solemn Music" (c.1633): "And to our highest fantasy present / That undisturbèd song of pure concent" (5–6).

LETTER TO A YOUNG GENTLEMAN WHO PROPOSES TO EMBRACE THE CAREER OF ART

With the agreeable frankness of youth, you address me on a point of some practical importance to yourself and (it is even conceivable) of some gravity to the world: Should you or should you not become an artist? It is one which you must decide entirely for yourself; all that I can do is to bring under your notice some of the materials of that decision; and I will begin, as I shall probably conclude also, by assuring you that all depends on the vocation.

To know what you like is the beginning of wisdom and of old age. Youth is wholly experimental. The essence and charm of that unquiet and delightful epoch is ignorance of self as well as ignorance of life. These two unknowns the young man brings together again and again, now in the airiest touch, now with a bitter hug; now with exquisite pleasure, now with cutting pain; but never with indifference, to which he is a total stranger, and never with that near kinsman of indifference, contentment. If he be a youth of dainty senses or a brain easily heated, the interest of this series of experiments grows upon him out of all proportion to the pleasure he receives. It is not beauty that he loves, nor pleasure that he seeks, though he may think so; his design and his sufficient reward is to verify his own existence and taste the variety of human fate. To him, before the razor-edge of curiosity is dulled, all that is not actual living and the hot chase of experience wears a face of a disgusting dryness difficult to recall in later days; or if there be any exception—and here destiny steps in—it is in those moments when, wearied or surfeited of the primary activity of the senses, he calls up before memory the image of transacted pains and pleasures. Thus it is that such an one shies from all cut-and-dry professions, and inclines insensibly toward that career of art which consists only in the tasting and recording of experience.

This, which is not so much a vocation for art as an impatience of all other honest trades, frequently exists alone; and so existing, it will pass gently away in the course of years. Emphatically, it is not to be regarded; it is not a vocation, but a temptation; and when your father the other day so fiercely and (in my view) so properly discouraged your ambition, he was recalling not improbably some similar passage in his own experience. For the temptation is perhaps nearly as common as the vocation is rare. But again we have vocations which are imperfect; we have men whose minds are bound up, not so much in any art, as in the general *ars artium*[1] and common base of all creative work; who will now dip into painting, and now study counterpoint, and anon will be inditing[2] a sonnet: all these with equal interest, all often with genuine knowledge. And of this temper, when it stands alone, I find it difficult to speak; but I should counsel such an one to take to letters, for in literature (which drags with so wide a net) all his information

1. Logic.
2. Writing.

may be found some day useful, and if he should go on as he has begun, and turn at last into the critic, he will have learned to use the necessary tools. Lastly we come to those vocations which are at once decisive and precise; to the men who are born with the love of pigments, the passion of drawing, the gift of music, or the impulse to create with words, just as other and perhaps the same men are born with the love of hunting, or the sea, or horses, or the turning-lathe.[3] These are predestined; if a man love the labour of any trade apart from any question of success or fame, the gods have called him. He may have the general vocation too: he may have a taste for all the arts, and I think he often has; but the mark of his calling is this laborious partiality for one, this inextinguishable zest in its technical successes, and (perhaps above all) a certain candour of mind, to take his very trifling enterprise with a gravity that would befit the cares of empire, and to think the smallest improvement worth accomplishing at any expense of time and industry. The book, the statue, the sonata, must be gone upon with the unreasoning good faith and the unflagging spirit of children at their play. *Is it worth doing?*—when it shall have occurred to any artist to ask himself that question, it is implicitly answered in the negative. It does not occur to the child as he plays at being a pirate on the dining-room sofa, nor to the hunter as he pursues his quarry; and the candour of the one and the ardour of the other should be united in the bosom of the artist.

If you recognise in yourself some such decisive taste, there is no room for hesitation: follow your bent. And observe (lest I should too much discourage you) that the disposition does not usually burn so brightly at the first, or rather not so constantly. Habit and practice sharpen gifts; the necessity of toil grows less disgusting, grows even welcome in the course of years; a small taste (if it be only genuine) waxes with indulgence into an exclusive passion.

3. A machine used by woodworkers and metalworkers to cut, sand, or engrave a rotating piece of material.

Enough, just now, if you can look back over a fair interval, and see that your chosen art has a little more than held its own among the thronging interests of youth. Time will do the rest, if devotion help it; and soon your every thought will be engrossed in that beloved occupation.

But even with devotion, you may remind me, even with unfaltering and delighted industry, many thousand artists spend their lives, if the result be regarded, utterly in vain: a thousand artists, and never one work of art. But the vast mass of mankind are incapable of doing anything reasonably well, art among the rest. The worthless artist would not improbably have been a quite incompetent baker. And the artist, even if he does not amuse the public, amuses himself; so that there will always be one man the happier for his vigils. This is the practical side of art: its inexpugnable[4] fortress for the true practitioner. The direct returns—the wages of the trade—are small, but the indirect—the wages of the life—are incalculably great. No other business offers a man his daily bread upon such joyful terms. The soldier and the explorer have moments of a worthier excitement, but they are purchased by cruel hardships and periods of tedium that beggar language. In the life of the artist there need be no hour without its pleasure. I take the author, with whose career I am best acquainted;[5] and it is true he works in a rebellious material, and that the act of writing is cramped and trying both to the eyes and the temper; but remark him in his study, when matter crowds upon him and words are not wanting—in what a continual series of small successes time flows by; with what a sense of power, as of one moving mountains, he marshals his petty characters; with what pleasures, both of the ear and eye, he sees his airy structure growing on the page; and how he labours in a craft to which the whole material of his life is tributary, and which opens a door to all his tastes, his loves, his

4. Impregnable.
5. Stevenson himself.

hatreds, and his convictions, so that what he writes is only what he longed to utter. He may have enjoyed many things in this big, tragic playground of the world; but what shall he have enjoyed more fully than a morning of successful work? Suppose it ill paid: the wonder is it should be paid at all. Other men pay, and pay dearly, for pleasures less desirable.

Nor will the practice of art afford you pleasure only; it affords besides an admirable training. For the artist works entirely upon honour. The public knows little or nothing of those merits in the quest of which you are condemned to spend the bulk of your endeavours. Merits of design, the merit of first-hand energy, the merit of a certain cheap accomplishment which a man of the artistic temper easily acquires—these they can recognise, and these they value. But to those more exquisite refinements of proficiency and finish, which the artist so ardently desires and so keenly feels, for which (in the vigorous words of Balzac) he must toil "like a miner buried in a landslip,"[6] for which, day after day, he recasts and revises and rejects—the gross mass of the public must be ever blind. To those lost pains, suppose you attain the highest pitch of merit, posterity may possibly do justice; suppose, as is so probable, you fail by even a hair's breadth of the highest, rest certain they shall never be observed. Under the shadow of this cold thought, alone in his studio, the artist must preserve from day to day his constancy to the ideal. It is this which makes his life noble; it is by this that the practice of his craft strengthens and matures his character; it is for this that even the serious countenance of the great emperor[7] was turned approvingly (if only for a moment) on the followers of Apollo,[8] and that sternly gentle voice bade the artist cherish his art.

And here there fall two warnings to be made. First, if you are to continue to be a law to yourself, you must beware of the first

6. From the novel *Cousin Bette* (1846) by Honoré de Balzac (1799–1850).
7. Augustus (63 BC – 14 AD).
8. Poets.

signs of laziness. This idealism in honesty can only be supported by perpetual effort; the standard is easily lowered; the artist who says "*It will do*" is on the downward path; three or four pot-boilers[9] are enough at times (above all at wrong times) to falsify a talent, and by the practice of journalism a man runs the risk of becoming wedded to cheap finish. This is the danger on the one side; there is not less upon the other. The consciousness of how much the artist is (and must be) a law to himself, debauches the small heads. Perceiving recondite merits very hard to attain, making or swallowing artistic formulae, or perhaps falling in love with some particular proficiency of his own, many artists forget the end of all art: to please. It is doubtless tempting to exclaim against the ignorant bourgeois; yet it should not be forgotten, it is he who is to pay us, and that (surely on the face of it) for services that he shall desire to have performed. Here also, if properly considered, there is a question of transcendental honesty. To give the public what they do not want, and yet expect to be supported: we have there a strange pretension, and yet not uncommon, above all with painters. The first duty in this world is for a man to pay his way; when that is quite accomplished, he may plunge into what eccentricity he likes; but emphatically not till then. Till then, he must pay assiduous court to the bourgeois who carries the purse. And if in the course of these capitulations he shall falsify his talent, it can never have been a strong one, and he will have preserved a better thing than talent—character. Or if he be of a mind so independent that he cannot stoop to this necessity, one course is yet open: he can desist from art, and follow some more manly way of life.

I speak of a more manly way of life, it is a point on which I must be frank. To live by a pleasure is not a high calling; it involves patronage, however veiled; it numbers the artist, however ambitious, along with dancing-girls and billiard-markers.[10] The

9. Works of art of dubious merit, created to make the artist money.
10. Pool sharks.

French have a romantic evasion[11] for one employment, and call its practitioners the Daughters of Joy.[12] The artist is of the same family, he is of the Sons of Joy, chose his trade to please himself, gains his livelihood by pleasing others, and has parted with something of the sterner dignity of man. Journals but a little while ago declaimed against the Tennyson peerage;[13] and this Son of Joy was blamed for condescension when he followed the example of Lord Lawrence and Lord Cairns and Lord Clyde.[14] The poet was more happily inspired; with a better modesty he accepted the honour; and anonymous journalists have not yet (if I am to believe them) recovered the vicarious disgrace to their profession. When it comes to their turn, these gentlemen can do themselves more justice; and I shall be glad to think of it; for to my barbarian eyesight, even Lord Tennyson looks somewhat out of place in that assembly. There should be no honours for the artist; he has already, in the practice of his art, more than his share of the rewards of life; the honours are pre-empted for other trades, less agreeable and perhaps more useful.

But the devil in these trades of pleasing is to fail to please. In ordinary occupations, a man offers to do a certain thing or to produce a certain article with a merely conventional accomplishment, a design in which (we may almost say) it is difficult to fail. But the artist steps forth out of the crowd and proposes to delight: an impudent design, in which it is impossible to fail without odious circumstances. The poor Daughter of Joy, carrying her smiles and finery quite unregarded through the crowd, makes a figure which it is impossible to recall without a wounding pity. She is the type of

11. Euphemism.
12. Prostitutes.
13. After twice declining the honor, Alfred Tennyson (1809–1892) accepted the hereditary title of Baron from Queen Victoria in 1884 and became a lord.
14. Lord John Lawrence (1811–1879), former Viceroy of India, was created a Baron in 1869; Lord Hugh McCalmont Cairns (1819–1885), Conservative politician, was created a Baron in 1867 and a Viscount in 1878; Colin Campbell, Lord Clyde (1792–1863), British Field Marshal, was created a Baron in 1858.

the unsuccessful artist. The actor, the dancer, and the singer must appear like her in person, and drain publicly the cup of failure. But though the rest of us escape this crowning bitterness of the pillory, we all court in essence the same humiliation. We all profess to be able to delight. And how few of us are! We all pledge ourselves to be able to continue to delight. And the day will come to each, and even to the most admired, when the ardour shall have declined and the cunning shall be lost, and he shall sit by his deserted booth ashamed. Then shall he see himself condemned to do work for which he blushes to take payment. Then (as if his lot were not already cruel) he must lie exposed to the gibes[15] of the wreckers of the press, who earn a little bitter bread by the condemnation of trash which they have not read, and the praise of excellence which they cannot understand.

And observe that this seems almost the necessary end at least of writers. "Les Blancs et les Bleus"[16] (for instance) is of an order of merit very different from "Le Vicomte de Bragelonne";[17] and if any gentleman can bear to spy upon the nakedness of "Castle Dangerous,"[18] his name I think is Ham:[19] let it be enough for the rest of us to read of it (not without tears) in the pages of Lockhart.[20] Thus in old age, when occupation and comfort are most needful, the writer must lay aside at once his pastime and his breadwinner. The painter indeed, if he succeed at all in engaging the attention of the public, gains great sums and can stand to his easel until a

15. Jeers.
16. *The Whites and the Blues* (1867), a novel by Alexandre Dumas (1802–1870).
17. The novel *The Vicomte of Bragelonne: Ten Years Later* (1847–50) is also by Dumas.
18. Published in 1831, *Castle Dangerous* is the last—and some say the weakest—of Walter Scott's novels.
19. Having discovered his father Noah in a compromising position, drunk and naked, Ham tells his brothers, whereupon Noah curses Ham's children (Genesis 9:20–27).
20. Stevenson is referring to John Gibson Lockhart (1794–1854), Scott's son-in-law, whose ten-volume biography *Life of Sir Walter Scott* (1837–39) describes the cognitive decline that the aging novelist suffered while working on *Castle Dangerous*.

great age without dishonourable failure. The writer has the double misfortune to be ill-paid while he can work, and to be incapable of working when he is old. It is thus a way of life which conducts directly to a false position.

For the writer (in spite of notorious examples to the contrary) must look to be ill-paid. Tennyson and Montépin[21] make handsome livelihoods; but we cannot all hope to be Tennyson, and we do not all perhaps desire to be Montépin. If you adopt an art to be your trade, weed your mind at the outset of all desire of money. What you may decently expect, if you have some talent and much industry, is such an income as a clerk will earn with a tenth or perhaps a twentieth of your nervous output. Nor have you the right to look for more; in the wages of the life, not in the wages of the trade, lies your reward; the work is here the wages. It will be seen I have little sympathy with the common lamentations of the artist class. Perhaps they do not remember the hire of the field labourer; or do they think no parallel will lie?[22] Perhaps they have never observed what is the retiring allowance of a field officer; or do they suppose their contributions to the arts of pleasing more important than the services of a colonel? Perhaps they forget on how little Millet[23] was content to live; or do they think, because they have less genius, they stand excused from the display of equal virtues? But upon one point there should be no dubiety: if a man be not frugal, he has no business in the arts. If he be not frugal, he steers directly

21. Xavier de Montépin (1823–1902), popular French novelist.

22. An allusion to the Parable of the Workers in the Vineyard in the Book of Matthew. A landowner hires laborers to work his field for a *denarius* (a silver coin) each. Throughout the day, he hires more laborers. At the end of the day, he pays all the laborers the same wage. When the men who had been working since morning complain, arguing that they deserve more, the landowner replies: "So the last shall be first, and the first last: for many be called, but few chosen" (Matthew 20:16). The lesson of the parable is that God will reward the faithful equally, whether they discover Him early in life, or late. Stevenson urges his readers to pursue a career in art for the love of art, not in anticipation of monetary gain.

23. The painter Jean-François Millet (1814–1875) was born poor in rural France. Many of his paintings depict peasant laborers toiling in the fields.

for that last tragic scene of *le vieux saltimbanque*;[24] if he be not frugal, he will find it hard to continue to be honest. Someday, when the butcher is knocking at the door, he may be tempted, he may be obliged, to turn out and sell a slovenly piece of work. If the obligation shall have arisen through no wantonness of his own, he is even to be commended; for words cannot describe how far more necessary it is that a man should support his family, than that he should attain to—or preserve—distinction in the arts. But if the pressure comes through his own fault, he has stolen, and stolen under trust, and stolen (which is the worst of all) in such a way that no law can reach him.

And now you may perhaps ask me, if the débutant artist is to have no thought of money, and if (as is implied) he is to expect no honours from the State, he may not at least look forward to the delights of popularity? Praise, you will tell me, is a savoury dish. And in so far as you may mean the countenance of other artists, you would put your finger on one of the most essential and enduring pleasures of the career of art. But in so far as you should have an eye to the commendations of the public or the notice of the newspapers, be sure you would but be cherishing a dream. It is true that in certain esoteric journals the author (for instance) is duly criticised, and that he is often praised a great deal more than he deserves, sometimes for qualities which he prided himself on eschewing, and sometimes by ladies and gentlemen who have denied themselves the privilege of reading his work. But if a man be sensitive to this wild praise, we must suppose him equally alive to that which often accompanies and always follows it—wild ridicule. A man may have done well for years, and then he may fail;

24. Baudelaire's prose-poem "Le vieux saltimbanque" ("The Old Mountebank"), published posthumously in 1869, is about his encounter with a peddler of quack remedies. Baudelaire sees in the broken man the fate of writers too dependent upon public approbation: "I have just seen the face of the aging man of letters, who has outlived the days when he was considered a brilliant entertainer; of the old friendless poet, with no family, no children, degraded by his misery and by public ingratitude, into whose booth an apathetic world no longer wants to go!"

he will hear of his failure. Or he may have done well for years, and still do well, but the critics may have tired of praising him, or there may have sprung up some new idol of the instant, some "dust a little gilt,"[25] to whom they now prefer to offer sacrifice. Here is the obverse and the reverse of that empty and ugly thing called popularity. Will any man suppose it worth the gaining?

25. An allusion to Shakespeare's *Troilus and Cressida* (c.1602):

> One touch of nature makes the whole world kin,
> That all with one consent praise newborn gauds,
> Though they are made and molded of things past,
> And give to dust that is a little gilt
> More laud than gilt o'erdusted. (3.3.174–78)

BEGGARS

I

In a pleasant, airy, uphill country, it was my fortune when I was young to make the acquaintance of a certain beggar. I call him beggar, though he usually allowed his coat and his shoes (which were open-mouthed, indeed) to beg for him. He was the wreck of an athletic man, tall, gaunt, and bronzed; far gone in consumption,[1] with that disquieting smile of the mortally stricken on his face; but still active afoot, still with the brisk military carriage, the ready military salute. Three ways led through this piece of country; and as I was inconstant in my choice, I believe he must often have awaited me in vain. But often enough, he caught me; often enough, from some place of ambush by the roadside, he would spring suddenly forth in the regulation attitude, and launching at once into his inconsequential talk, fall into step with me upon my farther course. "A fine morning, sir, though perhaps a trifle inclining to rain. I hope I see you well, sir. Why, no, sir, I don't feel as hearty myself as I could wish, but I am keeping about my ordinary. I am pleased to meet you on the road, sir. I assure you I quite look forward to one of our little conversations." He loved the sound of his own voice inordinately, and though (with something too offhand to call servility) he would always hasten to agree with

1. Tuberculosis.

anything you said, yet he could never suffer you to say it to an end. By what transition he slid to his favourite subject I have no memory; but we had never been long together on the way before he was dealing, in a very military manner, with the English poets. "Shelley was a fine poet, sir, though a trifle atheistical in his opinions. His 'Queen Mab,'[2] sir, is quite an atheistical work. Scott, sir, is not so poetical a writer. With the works of Shakespeare I am not so well acquainted, but he was a fine poet. Keats—John Keats, sir—he was a very fine poet." With such references, such trivial criticism, such loving parade of his own knowledge, he would beguile the road, striding forward uphill, his staff now clapped to the ribs of his deep, resonant chest, now swinging in the air with the remembered jauntiness of the private soldier; and all the while his toes looking out of his boots, and his shirt looking out of his elbows, and death looking out of his smile, and his big, crazy[3] frame shaken by accesses of cough.

He would often go the whole way home with me: often to borrow a book, and that book always a poet. Off he would march, to continue his mendicant rounds, with the volume slipped into the pocket of his ragged coat; and although he would sometimes keep it quite a while, yet it came always back again at last, not much the worse for its travels into beggardom. And in this way, doubtless, his knowledge grew and his glib, random criticism took a wider range. But my library was not the first he had drawn upon: at our first encounter, he was already brimful of Shelley and the atheistical "Queen Mab," and "Keats—John Keats, sir." And I have often wondered how he came by these acquirements; just as I often wondered how he fell to be a beggar. He had served through the Mutiny[4]—of which (like so many people) he could tell

2. *Queen Mab; A Philosophical Poem; With Notes* (1813) by Percy Bysshe Shelley (1792–1822).

3. Disorderly.

4. Known today as the Indian Rebellion of 1857, or India's First War of Independence, "the Mutiny," as the British called it in the nineteenth century, was an anti-imperial uprising by Indian soldiers against the rule of the British East India Company. It took the British eighteen months to suppress the rebellion.

practically nothing beyond the names of places, and that it was "difficult work, sir," and very hot, or that so-and-so was "a very fine commander, sir." He was far too smart a man to have remained a private; in the nature of things, he must have won his stripes. And yet here he was without a pension. When I touched on this problem, he would content himself with diffidently offering me advice. "A man should be very careful when he is young, sir. If you'll excuse me saying so, a spirited young gentleman like yourself, sir, should be very careful. I was perhaps a trifle inclined to atheistical opinions myself." For (perhaps with a deeper wisdom than we are inclined in these days to admit) he plainly bracketed agnosticism with beer and skittles.[5]

Keats—John Keats, sir—and Shelley were his favourite bards. I cannot remember if I tried him with Rossetti;[6] but I know his taste to a hair, and if ever I did, he must have doted on that author. What took him was a richness in the speech; he loved the exotic, the unexpected word; the moving cadence of a phrase; a vague sense of emotion (about nothing) in the very letters of the alphabet: the romance of language. His honest head was very nearly empty, his intellect like a child's; and when he read his favourite authors, he can almost never have understood what he was reading. Yet the taste was not only genuine, it was exclusive; I tried in vain to offer him novels; he would none of them; he cared for nothing but romantic language that he could not understand. The case may be commoner than we suppose. I am reminded of a lad who was laid in the next cot to a friend of mine in a public hospital, and who was no sooner installed than he sent out (perhaps with his last pence) for a cheap Shakespeare. My friend pricked up his ears; fell at once in talk with his new neighbour, and was ready, when the book arrived, to make a singular discovery. For this lover of great literature understood not one sentence out of twelve, and

5. A game similar to bowling.
6. Dante Gabriel Rossetti (1828–1882), British poet, painter and leader of the Pre-Raphaelite Brotherhood.

his favourite part was that of which he understood the least—the inimitable, mouth-filling rodomontade[7] of the ghost in *Hamlet*. It was a bright day in hospital when my friend expounded the sense of this beloved jargon: a task for which I am willing to believe my friend was very fit, though I can never regard it as an easy one. I know indeed a point or two, on which I would gladly question Mr. Shakespeare, that lover of big words, could he revisit the glimpses of the moon, or could I myself climb backward to the spacious days of Elizabeth. But in the second case, I should most likely pretermit[8] these questionings, and take my place instead in the pit at the Blackfriars[9], to hear the actor in his favourite part, playing up to Mr. Burbage,[10] and rolling out—as I seem to hear him—with a ponderous gusto—

> "Unhousel'd, disappointed, unanel'd."[11]

What a pleasant chance, if we could go there in a party! and what a surprise for Mr. Burbage, when the ghost received the honours of the evening!

As for my old soldier, like Mr. Burbage and Mr. Shakespeare, he is long since dead; and now lies buried, I suppose, and nameless and quite forgotten, in some poor city graveyard.—But not for me, you brave heart, have you been buried! For me, you are

7. Boastful talk.
8. Abandon.
9. A theater in sixteenth-century London.
10. Shakespeare is rumored to have acted the part of the Ghost in the first production of *Hamlet* in 1601. The famous Elizabethan actor Richard Burbage (1567–1619) played the Prince of Denmark.
11.

> Thus was I, sleeping, by a brother's hand
> Of life, of crown, of queen at once dispatched,
> Cut off even in the blossoms of my sin,
> Unhouseled, disappointed, unaneled,
> No reck'ning made, but sent to my account
> With all my imperfections on my head. (1.5.74–79)

still afoot, tasting the sun and air, and striding southward. By the groves of Comiston and beside the Hermitage of Braid, by the Hunters' Tryst, and where the curlews and plovers cry around Fairmilehead,[12] I see and hear you, stalwartly carrying your deadly sickness, cheerfully discoursing of uncomprehended poets.

II

The thought of the old soldier recalls that of another tramp, his counterpart. This was a little, lean, and fiery man, with the eyes of a dog and the face of a gipsy; whom I found one morning encamped with his wife and children and his grinder's wheel, beside the burn[13] of Kinnaird. To this beloved dell I went, at that time, daily; and daily the knife-grinder and I (for as long as his tent continued pleasantly to interrupt my little wilderness) sat on two stones, and smoked, and plucked grass, and talked to the tune of the brown water. His children were mere whelps, they fought and bit among the fern like vermin. His wife was a mere squaw; I saw her gather brush and tend the kettle, but she never ventured to address her lord while I was present. The tent was a mere gipsy hovel, like a sty for pigs. But the grinder himself had the fine self-sufficiency and grave politeness of the hunter and the savage; he did me the honours of this dell, which had been mine but the day before, took me far into the secrets of his life, and used me (I am proud to remember) as a friend.

Like my old soldier, he was far gone in the national complaint.[14] Unlike him, he had a vulgar taste in letters; scarce flying higher than the story papers; probably finding no difference, certainly seeking none, between Tannahill[15] and Burns; his noblest

12. Edinburgh suburbs.
13. Creek.
14. Tuberculosis.
15. Robert Tannahill (1774–1810), Scottish working-class poet.

thoughts, whether of poetry or music, adequately embodied in that somewhat obvious ditty,

> "Will ye gang, lassie, gang
> To the braes o' Balquhidder":[16]

—which is indeed apt to echo in the ears of Scottish children, and to him, in view of his experience, must have found a special directness of address. But if he had no fine sense of poetry in letters, he felt with a deep joy the poetry of life. You should have heard him speak of what he loved; of the tent pitched beside the talking water; of the stars overhead at night; of the blest return of morning, the peep of day over the moors, the awaking birds among the birches; how he abhorred the long winter shut in cities; and with what delight, at the return of the spring, he once more pitched his camp in the living out-of-doors. But we were a pair of tramps; and to you, who are doubtless sedentary and a consistent first-class passenger in life, he would scarce have laid himself so open;—to you, he might have been content to tell his story of a ghost—that of a buccaneer with his pistols as he lived—whom he had once encountered in a seaside cave near Buckie;[17] and that would have been enough, for that would have shown you the mettle of the man. Here was a piece of experience solidly and livingly built up in words, here was a story created, *teres atque rotundus.*[18]

And to think of the old soldier, that lover of the literary bards! He had visited stranger spots than any seaside cave; encountered men more terrible than any spirit; done and dared and suffered in that incredible, unsung epic of the Mutiny War; played his part with the field force of Delhi, beleaguering and beleaguered; shared in that enduring, savage anger and contempt of death and

16. From "Braes of Balquhidder," Tannahill's most famous poem.
17. A town in northern Scotland.
18. "both smooth and round"

decency that, for long months together, bedevil'd and inspired the army; was hurled to and fro in the battle-smoke of the assault; was there, perhaps, where Nicholson[19] fell; was there when the attacking column, with hell upon every side, found the soldier's enemy—strong drink,[20] and the lives of tens of thousands trembled in the scale, and the fate of the flag of England staggered. And of all this he had no more to say than "hot work, sir," or "the army suffered a great deal, sir," or "I believe General Wilson, sir, was not very highly thought of in the papers." His life was naught to him, the vivid pages of experience quite blank: in words his pleasure lay—melodious, agitated words—printed words, about that which he had never seen and was connatally[21] incapable of comprehending. We have here two temperaments face to face; both untrained, unsophisticated, surprised (we may say) in the egg; both boldly charactered:—that of the artist, the lover and artificer of words; that of the maker, the seeër, the lover and forger of experience. If the one had a daughter and the other had a son, and these married, might not some illustrious writer count descent from the beggar-soldier and the needy knife-grinder?

III

Everyone lives by selling something, whatever be his right to it. The burglar sells at the same time his own skill and courage and my silver plate (the whole at the most moderate figure) to a Jew receiver. The bandit sells the traveller an article of prime necessity: that traveller's life. And as for the old soldier, who stands for central mark to my capricious figures of eight, he dealt in a specialty; for he was the only beggar in the world who ever gave

19. British military officer John Nicholson (1821–1857) died from injuries sustained during the Siege of Delhi, a key battle in the Indian Rebellion of 1857. His charisma and heroism captured the imagination of the British public.
20. British soldiers looted liquor stores as they advanced on Delhi. A frustrated General Archdale Wilson (1803–1874) ordered all alcohol destroyed.
21. Congenitally.

me pleasure for my money. He had learned a school of manners in the barracks and had the sense to cling to it, accosting strangers with a regimental freedom, thanking patrons with a merely regimental difference, sparing you at once the tragedy of his position and the embarrassment of yours. There was not one hint about him of the beggar's emphasis, the outburst of revolting gratitude, the rant and cant, the "God bless you, Kind, Kind gentleman," which insults the smallness of your alms by disproportionate vehemence, which is so notably false, which would be so unbearable if it were true. I am sometimes tempted to suppose this reading of the beggar's part, a survival of the old days when Shakespeare was intoned upon the stage and mourners keened[22] beside the death-bed; to think that we cannot now accept these strong emotions unless they be uttered in the just note of life; nor (save in the pulpit) endure these gross conventions. They wound us, I am tempted to say, like mockery; the high voice of keening (as it yet lingers on) strikes in the face of sorrow like a buffet;[23] and the rant and cant of the staled beggar stirs in us a shudder of disgust. But the fact disproves these amateur opinions. The beggar lives by his knowledge of the average man. He knows what he is about when he bandages his head, and hires and drugs a babe, and poisons life with "Poor Mary Ann" or "Long, long ago";[24] he knows what he is about when he loads the critical ear and sickens the nice conscience with intolerable thanks; they know what they are about, he and his crew, when they pervade the slums of cities, ghastly parodies of suffering, hateful parodies of gratitude. This trade can scarce be called an imposition; it has been so blown upon with exposures; it flaunts its fraudulence so nakedly. We pay them as we pay those who show us, in huge exaggeration, the monsters of our drinking-water; or those who daily predict the fall of Britain. We pay them for the pain they inflict, pay them, and

22. Wailed.
23. Slap.
24. Pathos-filled folk songs.

wince, and hurry on. And truly there is nothing that can shake the conscience like a beggar's thanks; and that polity in which such protestations can be purchased for a shilling, seems no scene for an honest man.

Are there, then, we may be asked, no genuine beggars? And the answer is, Not one. My old soldier was a humbug like the rest; his ragged boots were, in the stage phrase, properties; whole boots were given him again and again, and always gladly accepted; and the next day, there he was on the road as usual, with toes exposed. His boots were his method; they were the man's trade; without his boots he would have starved; he did not live by charity, but by appealing to a gross taste in the public, which loves the limelight on the actor's face, and the toes out of the beggar's boots. There is a true poverty, which no one sees: a false and merely mimetic poverty, which usurps its place and dress, and lives and above all drinks, on the fruits of the usurpation. The true poverty does not go into the streets; the banker may rest assured, he has never put a penny in its hand. The self-respecting poor beg from each other; never from the rich. To live in the frock-coated ranks of life, to hear canting scenes of gratitude rehearsed for twopence, a man might suppose that giving was a thing gone out of fashion; yet it goes forward on a scale so great as to fill me with surprise. In the houses of the working classes, all day long there will be a foot upon the stair; all day long there will be a knocking at the doors; beggars come, beggars go, without stint, hardly with intermission, from morning till night; and meanwhile, in the same city and but a few streets off, the castles of the rich stand unsummoned. Get the tale of any honest tramp, you will find it was always the poor who helped him; get the truth from any workman who has met misfortunes, it was always next door that he would go for help, or only with such exceptions as are said to prove a rule; look at the course of the mimetic beggar, it is through the poor quarters that he trails his passage, showing his bandages to every window, piercing even to the attics with his nasal song. Here is a remarkable state of things in our Christian commonwealths, that the poor only should be asked to give.

IV

There is a pleasant tale of some worthless, phrasing Frenchman, who was taxed with ingratitude: "*Il faut savoir garder l'indépendance du cœur,*"[25] cried he. I own I feel with him. Gratitude without familiarity, gratitude otherwise than as a nameless element in a friendship, is a thing so near to hatred that I do not care to split the difference. Until I find a man who is pleased to receive obligations, I shall continue to question the tact of those who are eager to confer them. What an art it is, to give, even to our nearest friends! and what a test of manners to receive! How, upon either side, we smuggle away the obligation, blushing for each other; how bluff and dull we make the giver; how hasty, how falsely cheerful, the receiver! And yet an act of such difficulty and distress between near friends, it is supposed we can perform to a total stranger and leave the man transfixed with grateful emotions. The last thing you can do to a man is to burthen him with an obligation, and it is what we propose to begin with! But let us not be deceived: unless he is totally degraded to his trade, anger jars in his inside, and he grates his teeth at our gratuity.

We should wipe two words from our vocabulary: gratitude and charity. In real life, help is given out of friendship, or it is not valued; it is received from the hand of friendship, or it is resented. We are all too proud to take a naked gift: we must seem to pay it, if in nothing else, then with the delights of our society. Here, then, is the pitiful fix of the rich man; here is that needle's eye in which he

25. Loose translation: "One must maintain an independence of heart." The Frenchman was dandy, theater director and amateur magician Nestor Roqueplan (1805–1870), whose exact words were: "*L'ingratitude est l'indépendance du coeur*" ("Ingratitude is the heart's independence.").

stuck already in the days of Christ,[26] and still sticks today, firmer, if possible, than ever: that he has the money and lacks the love which should make his money acceptable. Here and now, just as of old in Palestine, he has the rich to dinner, it is with the rich that he takes his pleasure: and when his turn comes to be charitable, he looks in vain for a recipient. His friends are not poor, they do not want; the poor are not his friends, they will not take. To whom is he to give? Where to find—note this phrase—the Deserving Poor? Charity is (what they call) centralised; offices are hired; societies founded, with secretaries paid or unpaid: the hunt of the Deserving Poor goes merrily forward. I think it will take more than a merely human secretary to disinter that character. What! a class that is to be in want from no fault of its own, and yet greedily eager to receive from strangers; and to be quite respectable, and at the same time quite devoid of self-respect; and play the most delicate part of friendship, and yet never be seen; and wear the form of man, and yet fly in the face of all the laws of human nature:—and all this, in the hope of getting a belly-god Burgess[27] through a needle's eye! O, let him stick, by all means: and let his polity tumble in the dust; and let his epitaph and all his literature (of which my own works begin to form no inconsiderable part) be abolished even from the history of man! For a fool of this monstrosity of dulness, there can be no salvation: and the fool who looked for the elixir of life[28] was an angel of reason to the fool who looks for the Deserving Poor!

V

And yet there is one course which the unfortunate gentleman may take. He may subscribe to pay the taxes. There were the true charity, impartial and impersonal, cumbering none with obligation,

26. "I say unto you, It is easier for a camel to go through the eye of a needle, than for a rich man to enter into the kingdom of God" (Matthew 19:24).
27. A greedy bourgeois.
28. A magic potion that grants the drinker immortality.

helping all. There were a destination for loveless gifts; there were the way to reach the pocket of the deserving poor, and yet save the time of secretaries! But, alas! there is no colour of romance in such a course; and people nowhere demand the picturesque so much as in their virtues.

ORDERED SOUTH

By a curious irony of fate, the places to which we are sent when health deserts us are often singularly beautiful. Often, too, they are places we have visited in former years, or seen briefly in passing by, and kept ever afterwards in pious memory; and we please ourselves with the fancy that we shall repeat many vivid and pleasurable sensations, and take up again the thread of our enjoyment in the same spirit as we let it fall. We shall now have an opportunity of finishing many pleasant excursions, interrupted of yore before our curiosity was fully satisfied. It may be that we have kept in mind, during all these years, the recollection of some valley into which we have just looked down for a moment before we lost sight of it in the disorder of the hills; it may be that we have lain awake at night, and agreeably tantalized ourselves with the thought of corners we had never turned, or summits we had all but climbed: we shall now be able, as we tell ourselves, to complete all these unfinished pleasures, and pass beyond the barriers that confined our recollections.

The promise is so great, and we are all so easily led away when hope and memory are both in one story, that I dare say the sick man is not very inconsolable when he receives sentence of banishment, and is inclined to regard his ill-health as not the least fortunate accident of his life. Nor is he immediately undeceived. The stir and speed of the journey, and the restlessness that goes to bed with him as he tries to sleep between two days of noisy progress, fever him, and stimulate his dull nerves into something of their old quickness and sensibility. And so he can enjoy the faint autumnal splendour of the landscape, as he sees hill and plain, vineyard and forest, clad in one wonderful glory of fairy gold, which the first great winds of winter will transmute, as in the fable, into withered leaves. And so too he can enjoy the admirable brevity and simplicity of such little glimpses of country and country ways as flash upon him through the windows of the train; little glimpses that have a character all their own; sights seen as a travelling swallow might see them from the wing, or Iris[1] as she went abroad over the land on some Olympian errand. Here and there, indeed, a few children huzzah and wave their hands to the express; but for the most part, it is an interruption too brief and isolated to attract much notice; the sheep do not cease from browsing;[2] a girl sits balanced on the projecting tiller of a canal boat, so precariously that it seems as if a fly or the splash of a leaping fish would be enough to overthrow the dainty equilibrium, and yet all these hundreds of tons of coal and wood and iron have been precipitated roaring past her very ear, and there is not a start, not a tremor, not a turn of the averted head, to indicate that she has been even conscious of its passage. Herein, I think, lies the chief attraction of railway travel. The speed is so easy, and the train disturbs so little the scenes through which it takes us, that our heart becomes full of the placidity and stillness of the country; and while the body is borne forward in the flying chain of carriages, the thoughts alight, as the humour moves them, at unfrequented stations; they make haste up the poplar alley that leads toward the town; they are left behind with the signalman as, shading his eyes with his hand, he watches the long train sweep away into the golden distance.

1. Iris the rainbow, messenger of the gods.
2. Grazing.

Moreover, there is still before the invalid the shock of wonder and delight with which he will learn that he has passed the indefinable line that separates South from North. And this is an uncertain moment; for sometimes the consciousness is forced upon him early, on the occasion of some slight association, a colour, a flower, or a scent; and sometimes not until, one fine morning, he wakes up with the southern sunshine peeping through the *persiennes*,[3] and the southern patois confusedly audible below the windows. Whether it come early or late, however, this pleasure will not end with the anticipation, as do so many others of the same family. It will leave him wider awake than it found him, and give a new significance to all he may see for many days to come. There is something in the mere name of the South that carries enthusiasm along with it. At the sound of the word, he pricks up his ears; he becomes as anxious to seek out beauties and to get by heart the permanent lines and character of the landscape, as if he had been told that it was all his own—an estate out of which he had been kept unjustly, and which he was now to receive in free and full possession. Even those who have never been there before feel as if they had been; and everybody goes comparing, and seeking for the familiar, and finding it with such ecstasies of recognition, that one would think they were coming home after a weary absence, instead of travelling hourly farther abroad.

It is only after he is fairly arrived and settled down in his chosen corner, that the invalid begins to understand the change that has befallen him. Everything about him is as he had remembered, or as he had anticipated. Here, at his feet, under his eyes, are the olive gardens and the blue sea. Nothing can change the eternal magnificence of form of the naked Alps behind Mentone;[4] nothing, not even the crude curves of the railway, can utterly deform the suavity of contour of one bay after another along the whole

3. Exterior window shutters.
4. Menton.

reach of the Riviera. And of all this, he has only a cold head-knowledge that is divorced from enjoyment. He recognizes with his intelligence that this thing and that thing is beautiful, while in his heart of hearts he has to confess that it is not beautiful for him. It is in vain that he spurs his discouraged spirit; in vain that he chooses out points of view, and stands there, looking with all his eyes, and waiting for some return of the pleasure that he remembers in other days, as the sick folk may have awaited the coming of the angel at the pool of Bethesda.[5] He is like an enthusiast leading about with him a stolid, indifferent tourist. There is someone by who is out of sympathy with the scene, and is not moved up to the measure of the occasion; and that someone is himself. The world is disenchanted for him. He seems to himself to touch things with muffled hands, and to see them through a veil. His life becomes a palsied fumbling after notes that are silent when he has found and struck them. He cannot recognize that this phlegmatic and unimpressionable body with which he now goes burthened, is the same that he knew heretofore so quick and delicate and alive.

He is tempted to lay the blame on the very softness and amenity of the climate, and to fancy that in the rigours of the winter at home, these dead emotions would revive and flourish. A longing for the brightness and silence of fallen snow seizes him at such times. He is homesick for the hale rough weather; for the tracery of the frost upon his window-panes at morning, the reluctant descent of the first flakes, and the white roofs relieved against the sombre sky. And yet the stuff of which these yearnings are made is of the flimsiest: if but the thermometer fall a little below its ordinary Mediterranean level, or a wind come down from the snow-clad Alps behind, the spirit of his fancies changes upon the instant, and many a doleful vignette of the grim wintry streets at home returns to him, and begins to haunt his memory. The

5. When an angel stirred the waters of this pool in ancient Jerusalem, "whosoever . . . stepped in was made whole of whatsoever disease he had" (John 5:4).

hopeless, huddled attitude of tramps in doorways; the flinching gait of barefoot children on the icy pavement; the sheen of the rainy streets towards afternoon; the meagre anatomy of the poor defined by the clinging of wet garments; the high canorous[6] note of the North-easter on days when the very houses seem to stiffen with cold: these, and such as these, crowd back upon him, and mockingly substitute themselves for the fanciful winter scenes with which he had pleased himself a while before. He cannot be glad enough that he is where he is. If only the others could be there also; if only those tramps could lie down for a little in the sunshine, and those children warm their feet, this once, upon a kindlier earth; if only there were no cold anywhere, and no nakedness, and no hunger; if only it were as well with all men as it is with him!

For it is not altogether ill with the invalid, after all. If it is only rarely that anything penetrates vividly into his numbed spirit, yet, when anything does, it brings with it a joy that is all the more poignant for its very rarity. There is something pathetic in these occasional returns of a glad activity of heart. In his lowest hours he will be stirred and awakened by many such; and they will spring perhaps from very trivial sources; as a friend once said to me, the "spirit of delight" comes often on small wings. For the pleasure that we take in beautiful nature is essentially capricious. It comes sometimes when we least look for it; and sometimes, when we expect it most certainly, it leaves us to gape joylessly for days together, in the very home-land of the beautiful. We may have passed a place a thousand times and one; and on the thousand and second it will be transfigured, and stand forth in a certain splendour of reality from the dull circle of surroundings; so that we see it "with a child's first pleasure," as Wordsworth saw the daffodils by the lake-side.[7] And if this falls out capriciously with the

6. Musical.
7. See Wordsworth's "I Wandered Lonely as a Cloud" (1802).

healthy, how much more so with the invalid. Someday he will find his first violet, and be lost in pleasant wonder, by what alchemy the cold earth of the clods, and the vapid air and rain, can be transmuted into colour so rich and odour so touchingly sweet. Or perhaps he may see a group of washerwomen relieved, on a spit of shingle, against the blue sea, or a meeting of flower-gatherers in the tempered daylight of an olive-garden; and something significant or monumental in the grouping, something in the harmony of faint colour that is always characteristic of the dress of these southern women, will come home to him unexpectedly, and awake in him that satisfaction with which we tell ourselves that we are the richer by one more beautiful experience. Or it may be something even slighter: as when the opulence of the sunshine, which somehow gets lost and fails to produce its effect on the large scale, is suddenly revealed to him by the chance isolation—as he changes the position of his sunshade—of a yard or two of roadway with its stones and weeds. And then, there is no end to the infinite variety of the olive-yards themselves. Even the colour is indeterminate and continually shifting: now you would say it was green, now grey, now blue; now tree stands above tree, like "cloud on cloud," massed into filmy indistinctness; and now, at the wind's will, the whole sea of foliage is shaken and broken up with little momentary silverings and shadows. But everyone sees the world in his own way. To some the glad moment may have arrived on other provocations; and their recollection may be most vivid of the stately gait of women carrying burthens on their heads; of tropical effects, with canes and naked rock and sunlight; of the relief of cypresses; of the troubled, busy-looking groups of sea-pines, that seem always as if they were being wielded and swept together by a whirlwind; of the air coming, laden with virginal perfumes, over the myrtles and the scented underwood; of the empurpled hills standing up, solemn and sharp, out of the green-gold air of the east at evening.

There go many elements, without doubt, to the making of one such moment of intense perception; and it is on the happy agreement of these many elements, on the harmonious vibration of many nerves, that the whole delight of the moment must depend. Who can forget how, when he has chanced upon some attitude of complete restfulness, after long uneasy rolling to and fro on grass or heather, the whole fashion of the landscape has been changed for him, as though the sun had just broken forth, or a great artist had only then completed, by some cunning touch, the composition of the picture? And not only a change of posture—a snatch of perfume, the sudden singing of a bird, the freshness of some pulse of air from an invisible sea, the light shadow of a travelling cloud, the merest nothing that sends a little shiver along the most infinitesimal nerve of a man's body—not one of the least of these but has a hand somehow in the general effect, and brings some refinement of its own into the character of the pleasure we feel.

And if the external conditions are thus varied and subtle, even more so are those within our own bodies. No man can find out the world, says Solomon, from beginning to end, because the world is in his heart; and so it is impossible for any of us to understand, from beginning to end, that agreement of harmonious circumstances that creates in us the highest pleasure of admiration, precisely because some of these circumstances are hidden from us forever in the constitution of our own bodies. After we have reckoned up all that we can see or hear or feel, there still remains to be taken into account some sensibility more delicate than usual in the nerves affected, or some exquisite refinement in the architecture of the brain, which is indeed to the sense of the beautiful as the eye or the ear to the sense of hearing or sight. We admire splendid views and great pictures; and yet what is truly admirable is rather the mind within us, that gathers together these scattered details for its delight, and makes out of certain colours, certain distributions of graduated light and darkness, that intelligible whole which alone we call a picture or a view. Hazlitt,[8] relating in one of his essays how he went on foot from one great man's house to another's in search of works of art, begins suddenly to triumph over these noble or wealthy owners, because he was more capable of enjoying their costly possessions than they were; because they had paid the money and he had received the pleasure.[9] And the occasion is a fair one for self-complacency. While the one man was working to be able to buy the picture, the other was working to be able to enjoy the picture. An inherited aptitude will have been diligently improved in either case; only the one man has made for himself a fortune, and the other has made for himself a living spirit. It is a fair occasion for self-complacency, I repeat, when the event shows a man to have chosen the better part, and laid out his life more wisely, in the long run, than those who have credit for most wisdom. And yet even this is not a good unmixed; and like all other possessions, although in a less degree, the possession of a brain that has been thus improved and cultivated, and made into the prime organ of a man's enjoyment, brings with it certain inevitable cares and disappointments. The happiness of such an one comes to depend greatly upon those fine shades of sensation that heighten and harmonize the coarser elements of beauty. And thus a degree of nervous prostration, that to other men would be hardly disagreeable, is enough to overthrow for him the whole fabric of his life, to take, except at rare moments, the edge off his pleasures, and to meet him wherever he goes with failure, and the sense of want, and disenchantment of the world and life.

---

8. William Hazlitt (1778–1830), English literary critic, painter and essayist.
9. From Hazlitt's "On the Pleasure of Painting" (1844):

> The young artist makes a pilgrimage to each of these places, eyes them wistfully at a distance, "bosomed high in tufted trees," and feels an interest in them of which the owner is scare conscious. . . . He furnishes out the chambers of the mind from the spoils of time, picks and chooses which should have the best places—nearest his heart. He goes away richer than he came, richer than the possessor. . . .

It is not in such numbness of spirit only that the life of the invalid resembles a premature old age. Those excursions that he had promised himself to finish prove too long or too arduous for his feeble body; and the barrier-hills are as impassable as ever. Many a white town that sits far out on the promontory, many a comely fold of wood on the mountain side, beckons and allures his imagination day after day, and is yet as inaccessible to his feet as the clefts and gorges of the clouds. The sense of distance grows upon him wonderfully; and after some feverish efforts and the fretful uneasiness of the first few days, he falls contentedly in with the restrictions of his weakness. His narrow round becomes pleasant and familiar to him as the cell to a contented prisoner. Just as he has fallen already out of the mid race of active life, he now falls out of the little eddy that circulates in the shallow waters of the sanatorium. He sees the country people come and go about their everyday affairs, the foreigners stream out in goodly pleasure parties; the stir of man's activity is all about him, as he suns himself inertly in some sheltered corner; and he looks on with a patriarchal impersonality of interest, such as a man may feel when he pictures to himself the fortunes of his remote descendants, or the robust old age of the oak he has planted over-night.

In this falling aside, in this quietude and desertion of other men, there is no inharmonious prelude to the last quietude and desertion of the grave; in this dulness of the senses there is a gentle preparation for the final insensibility of death. And to him the idea of mortality comes in a shape less violent and harsh than is its wont, less as an abrupt catastrophe than as a thing of infinitesimal gradation, and the last step on a long decline of way. As we turn to and fro in bed, and every moment the movements grow feebler and smaller and the attitude more restful and easy, until sleep overtakes us at a stride and we move no more, so desire after desire leaves him; day by day his strength decreases, and the circle of his activity grows ever narrower; and he feels, if he is to be thus tenderly weaned from the passion of life, thus gradually inducted into the slumber of death, that when at last the end comes, it will come quietly and fitly. If anything is to reconcile poor spirits to the coming of the last enemy, surely it should be such a mild approach as this; not to hale us forth with violence, but to persuade us from a place we have no further pleasure in. It is not so much, indeed, death that approaches as life that withdraws and withers up from round about him. He has outlived his own usefulness, and almost his own enjoyment; and if there is to be no recovery; if never again will he be young and strong and passionate, if the actual present shall be to him always like a thing read in a book or remembered out of the far-away past; if, in fact, this be veritably nightfall, he will not wish greatly for the continuance of a twilight that only strains and disappoints the eyes, but steadfastly await the perfect darkness. He will pray for Medea:[10] when she comes, let her either rejuvenate or slay.

And yet the ties that still attach him to the world are many and kindly. The sight of children has a significance for him such as it may have for the aged also, but not for others. If he has been used to feel humanely, and to look upon life somewhat more widely than from the narrow loophole of personal pleasure and advancement, it is strange how small a portion of his thoughts will be changed or embittered by this proximity of death. He knows that already, in English counties, the sower follows the ploughman up the face of the field, and the rooks follow the sower; and he knows also that he may not live to go home again and see the corn spring and ripen, and be cut down at last, and brought home with gladness. And yet the future of this harvest, the continuance of drought or the coming of rain unseasonably, touch him as sensibly as ever. For he has long been used to wait with interest the issue of events in which his own concern was nothing; and to be joyful in a plenty, and sorrowful for a famine, that did not increase or diminish, by one half loaf, the equable sufficiency of his own supply. Thus there

10. In Greek mythology, Medea is a sorceress who slays her own children.

remain unaltered all the disinterested hopes for mankind and a better future which have been the solace and inspiration of his life. These he has set beyond the reach of any fate that only menaces himself; and it makes small difference whether he die five thousand years, or five thousand and fifty years, before the good epoch for which he faithfully labours. He has not deceived himself; he has known from the beginning that he followed the pillar of fire and cloud,[11] only to perish himself in the wilderness, and that it was reserved for others to enter joyfully into possession of the land. And so, as everything grows greyer and quieter about him, and slopes towards extinction, these unfaded visions accompany his sad decline, and follow him, with friendly voices and hopeful words, into the very vestibule of death. The desire of love or of fame scarcely moved him, in his days of health, more strongly than these generous aspirations move him now; and so life is carried forward beyond life, and a vista kept open for the eyes of hope, even when his hands grope already on the face of the impassable.

Lastly, he is bound tenderly to life by the thought of his friends; or shall we not say rather, that by their thought for him, by their unchangeable solicitude and love, he remains woven into the very stuff of life, beyond the power of bodily dissolution to undo? In a thousand ways will he survive and be perpetuated. Much of Etienne de la Boétie[12] survived during all the years in which Montaigne continued to converse with him on the pages of the ever-delightful essays. Much of what was truly Goethe[13] was dead already when he revisited places that knew him no more, and found no better consolation than the promise of his own verses, that soon he too would be at rest. Indeed, when we think of what

11. "And the LORD went before them by day in a pillar of a cloud, to lead them the way; and by night in a pillar of fire, to give them light" (Exodus 13:21).
12. Étienne de La Boétie (1530–1563), French judge and intimate friend of philosopher Michel de Montaigne (1533–1592), whose writings on friendship were inspired by their relationship.
13. Johann Wolfgang von Goethe (1749–1832), German intellectual, statesman and writer.

it is that we most seek and cherish, and find most pride and pleasure in calling ours, it will sometimes seem to us as if our friends, at our decease, would suffer loss more truly than ourselves. As a monarch who should care more for the outlying colonies he knows on the map or through the report of his vicegerents,[14] than for the trunk of his empire under his eyes at home, are we not more concerned about the shadowy life that we have in the hearts of others, and that portion in their thoughts and fancies which, in a certain far-away sense, belongs to us, than about the real knot of our identity—that central metropolis of self, of which alone we are immediately aware—or the diligent service of arteries and veins, and infinitesimal activity of ganglia, which we know (as we know a proposition in Euclid)[15] to be the source and substance of the whole? At the death of everyone whom we love, some fair and honourable portion of our existence falls away, and we are dislodged from one of these dear provinces; and they are not, perhaps, the most fortunate who survive a long series of such impoverishments, till their life and influence narrow gradually into the meagre limit of their own spirits, and death, when he comes at last, can destroy them at one blow.

NOTE. —To this essay I must in honesty append a word or two of qualification; for this is one of the points on which a slightly greater age teaches us a slightly different wisdom:

A youth delights in generalities, and keeps loose from particular obligations; he jogs on the footpath way, himself pursuing butterflies, but courteously lending his applause to the advance of the human species and the coming of the kingdom of justice and love. As he grows older, he begins to think more narrowly of man's action in the general, and perhaps more arrogantly of

14. The administrative deputies of a monarch.
15. Euclid, ancient Greek mathematician and author of *Elements* (c.300 BC), a treatise on geometry.

his own in the particular. He has not that same unspeakable trust in what he would have done had he been spared, seeing finally that that would have been little; but he has a far higher notion of the blank that he will make by dying. A young man feels himself one too many in the world; his is a painful situation: he has no calling; no obvious utility; no ties, but to his parents, and these he is sure to disregard. I do not think that a proper allowance has been made for this true cause of suffering in youth; but by the mere fact of a prolonged existence, we outgrow either the fact or else the feeling. Either we become so callously accustomed to our own useless figure in the world, or else—and this, thank God, in the majority of cases—we so collect about us the interest or the love of our fellows, so multiply our effective part in the affairs of life, that we need to entertain no longer the question of our right to be.

And so in the majority of cases, a man who fancies himself dying, will get cold comfort from the very youthful view expressed in this essay. He, as a living man, has some to help, some to love, some to correct; it may be, some to punish. These duties cling, not upon humanity, but upon the man himself. It is he, not another, who is one woman's son and a second woman's husband and a third woman's father. That life which began so small, has now grown, with a myriad filaments, into the lives of others. It is not indispensable; another will take the place and shoulder the discharged responsibility; but the better the man and the nobler his purposes, the more will he be tempted to regret the extinction of his powers and the deletion of his personality. To have lived a generation is not only to have grown at home in that perplexing medium, but to have assumed innumerable duties. To die at such an age, has, for all but the entirely base, something of the air of a betrayal. A man does not only reflect upon what he might have done in a future that is never to be his; but beholding himself so early a deserter from the fight, he eats his heart for the good he might have done already. To have been so useless and now to lose all hope of being useful any more—there it is that death and memory assail him. And even if mankind shall go on, founding heroic cities, practising heroic virtues, rising steadily from strength to strength; even if his work shall be fulfilled, his friends consoled, his wife remarried by a better than he; how shall this alter, in one jot, his estimation of a career which was his only business in this world, which was so fitfully pursued, and which is now so ineffectively to end?

CHILD'S PLAY

The regret we have for our childhood is not wholly justifiable: so much a man may lay down without fear of public ribaldry; for although we shake our heads over the change, we are not unconscious of the manifold advantages of our new state. What we lose in generous impulse, we more than gain in the habit of generously watching others; and the capacity to enjoy Shakespeare may balance a lost aptitude for playing at soldiers. Terror is gone out of our lives, moreover; we no longer see the devil in the bed-curtains nor lie awake to listen to the wind. We go to school no more; and if we have only exchanged one drudgery for another (which is by no means sure), we are set free for ever from the daily fear of chastisement. And yet a great change has overtaken us; and although we do not enjoy ourselves less, at least we take our pleasure differently. We need pickles nowadays to make Wednesday's cold mutton please our Friday's appetite; and I can remember the time when to call it red venison, and tell myself a hunter's story, would have made it more palatable than the best of sauces. To the grown person, cold mutton is cold mutton all the world over; not all the mythology ever invented by man will make it better or worse to him; the broad fact, the clamant[1] reality, of the mutton carries away before it such seductive figments.

1. Glaring.

But for the child it is still possible to weave an enchantment over eatables; and if he has but read of a dish in a storybook, it will be heavenly manna to him for a week.

If a grown man does not like eating and drinking and exercise, if he is not something positive[2] in his tastes, it means he has a feeble body and should have some medicine; but children may be pure spirits, if they will, and take their enjoyment in a world of moonshine. Sensation does not count for so much in our first years as afterwards; something of the swaddling numbness of infancy clings about us; we see and touch and hear through a sort of golden mist. Children, for instance, are able enough to see, but they have no great faculty for looking; they do not use their eyes for the pleasure of using them, but for by-ends of their own; and the things I call to mind seeing most vividly were not beautiful in themselves, but merely interesting or enviable to me as I thought they might be turned to practical account in play. Nor is the sense of touch so clean and poignant in children as it is in a man. If you will turn over your old memories, I think the sensations of this sort you remember will be somewhat vague, and come to not much more than a blunt, general sense of heat on summer days, or a blunt, general sense of well-being in bed. And here, of course, you will understand pleasurable sensations; for overmastering pain—the most deadly and tragical element in life, and the true commander of man's soul and body—alas! pain has its own way with all of us; it breaks in, a rude visitant, upon the fairy garden where the child wanders in a dream, no less surely than it rules upon the field of battle, or sends the immortal war-god[3] whimpering to his father; and innocence, no more than philosophy, can protect us from this sting. As for taste, when we bear in mind the excesses of unmitigated sugar which delight a youthful palate, "it

2. Physical.
3. Ares, Greek god of war, was viewed as psychologically unstable by his father Zeus, as well as by the Greeks.

is surely no very cynical asperity"[4] to think taste a character of the maturer growth. Smell and hearing are perhaps more developed; I remember many scents, many voices, and a great deal of spring singing in the woods. But hearing is capable of vast improvement as a means of pleasure; and there is all the world between gaping wonderment at the jargon of birds, and the emotion with which a man listens to articulate music.

At the same time, and step by step with this increase in the definition and intensity of what we feel which accompanies our growing age, another change takes place in the sphere of intellect, by which all things are transformed and seen through theories and associations as through coloured windows. We make to ourselves day by day, out of history, and gossip, and economical speculations, and God knows what, a medium in which we walk and through which we look abroad. We study shop windows with other eyes than in our childhood, never to wonder, not always to admire, but to make and modify our little incongruous theories about life. It is no longer the uniform of a soldier that arrests our attention; but perhaps the flowing carriage of a woman, or perhaps a countenance that has been vividly stamped with passion and carries an adventurous story written in its lines. The pleasure of surprise is passed away; sugar loaves and water-carts[5] seem mighty tame to encounter; and we walk the streets to make

4. An allusion to Samuel Johnson's indignant letter (dated February 7, 1755) to the Earl of Chesterfield, in which he declines the aristocrat's belated offer of patronage. See Boswell's *The Life of Dr. Johnson* (1791):

> The notice which you have been pleased to take of my labours, had it been early had been kind, but it has been delayed till I am indifferent, and cannot enjoy it; till I am solitary, and cannot impart it; till I am known, and do not want it. I hope it is no very cynical asperity, not to confess obligations where no benefit has been received, or to be unwilling that the Publick should consider me as owing that to a Patron, which Providence has enabled me to do for myself.

5. In the days before piped water, the horse-drawn water-cart delivered water to the cisterns of middle-class customers.

romances and to sociologise. Nor must we deny that a good many of us walk them solely for the purposes of transit or in the interest of a livelier digestion. These, indeed, may look back with mingled thoughts upon their childhood, but the rest are in a better case; they know more than when they were children, they understand better, their desires and sympathies answer more nimbly to the provocation of the senses, and their minds are brimming with interest as they go about the world.

According to my contention, this is a flight to which children cannot rise. They are wheeled in perambulators or dragged about by nurses in a pleasing stupor. A vague, faint, abiding wonderment possesses them. Here and there some specially remarkable circumstance, such as a water-cart or a guardsman, fairly penetrates into the seat of thought and calls them, for half a moment, out of themselves; and you may see them, still towed forward sideways by the inexorable nurse as by a sort of destiny, but still staring at the bright object in their wake. It may be some minutes before another such moving spectacle reawakens them to the world in which they dwell. For other children, they almost invariably show some intelligent sympathy. "There is a fine fellow making mud pies," they seem to say; "that I can understand, there is some sense in mud pies." But the doings of their elders, unless where they are speakingly[6] picturesque or recommend themselves by the quality of being easily imitable, they let them go over their heads (as we say) without the least regard. If it were not for this perpetual imitation, we should be tempted to fancy they despised us outright, or only considered us in the light of creatures brutally strong and brutally silly; among whom they condescended to dwell in obedience like a philosopher at a barbarous court. At times, indeed, they display an arrogance of disregard that is truly staggering. Once, when I was groaning aloud with physical pain, a young gentleman came into the room and nonchalantly inquired if

6. Obviously.

I had seen his bow and arrow. He made no account of my groans, which he accepted, as he had to accept so much else, as a piece of the inexplicable conduct of his elders; and, like a wise young gentleman, he would waste no wonder on the subject. Those elders, who care so little for rational enjoyment, and are even the enemy of rational enjoyment for others, he had accepted without understanding and without complaint, as the rest of us accept the scheme of the universe.

We grown people can tell ourselves a story, give and take strokes until the bucklers[7] ring, ride far and fast, marry, fall, and die; all the while sitting quietly by the fire or lying prone in bed. This is exactly what a child cannot do, or does not do, at least, when he can find anything else. He works all with lay figures and stage properties. When his story comes to the fighting, he must rise, get something by way of a sword and have a set-to with a piece of furniture, until he is out of breath. When he comes to ride with the king's pardon, he must bestride a chair, which he will so hurry and belabour and on which he will so furiously demean himself, that the messenger will arrive, if not bloody with spurring, at least fiery red with haste. If his romance involves an accident upon a cliff, he must clamber in person about the chest of drawers and fall bodily upon the carpet, before his imagination is satisfied. Lead soldiers, dolls, all toys, in short, are in the same category and answer the same end. Nothing can stagger a child's faith; he accepts the clumsiest substitutes and can swallow the most staring incongruities. The chair he has just been besieging as a castle, or valiantly cutting to the ground as a dragon, is taken away for the accommodation of a morning visitor, and he is nothing abashed; he can skirmish by the hour with a stationary coal-scuttle;[8] in the midst of the enchanted pleasance, he can see, without sensible shock, the gardener soberly digging potatoes for the day's dinner. He can make abstraction of whatever

7. Shields.
8. Bucket for carrying coal.

does not fit into his fable; and he puts his eyes into his pocket, just as we hold our noses in an unsavoury lane. And so it is, that although the ways of children cross with those of their elders in a hundred places daily, they never go in the same direction nor so much as lie in the same element. So may the telegraph wires intersect the line of the highroad, or so might a landscape painter and a bagman[9] visit the same country, and yet move in different worlds.

People, struck with these spectacles, cry aloud about the power of imagination in the young. Indeed, there may be two words to that. It is, in some ways, but a pedestrian fancy that the child exhibits. It is the grown people who make the nursery stories; all the children do is jealously preserve the text. One out of a dozen reasons why "Robinson Crusoe"[10] should be so popular with youth, is that it hits their level in this matter to a nicety; Crusoe was always at makeshifts and had, in so many words, to *play* at a great variety of professions; and then the book is all about tools, and there is nothing that delights a child so much. Hammers and saws belong to a province of life that positively calls for imitation. The juvenile lyrical drama,[11] surely of the most ancient Thespian model, wherein the trades of mankind are successively simulated to the running burthen "On a cold and frosty morning,"[12] gives a good instance of the artistic taste in children. And this need for overt action and lay figures[13] testifies to a defect in the child's imagination which prevents him from carrying out

---

9. Traveling salesman.
10. Daniel Defoe's 1719 novel about an English castaway on a tropical island.
11. Pantomime.
12. The refrain in the nursery rhyme "Here We Go Round the Mulberry Bush":

> Here we go round the mulberry bush,
> The mulberry bush,
> The mulberry bush.
> Here we go round the mulberry bush
> On a cold and frosty morning.

13. Artists' dummies.

his novels[14] in the privacy of his own heart. He does not yet know enough of the world and men. His experience is incomplete. That stage-wardrobe and scene-room that we call the memory is so ill provided, that he can overtake few combinations and body out few stories, to his own content, without some external aid. He is at the experimental stage; he is not sure how one would feel in certain circumstances; to make sure, he must come as near trying it as his means permit. And so here is young heroism with a wooden sword, and mothers practise their kind vocation over a bit of jointed stick. It may be laughable enough just now; but it is these same people and these same thoughts, that not long hence, when they are on the theatre of life, will make you weep and tremble. For children think very much the same thoughts, and dream the same dreams, as bearded men and marriageable women. No one is more romantic. Fame and honour, the love of young men and the love of mothers, the business man's pleasure in method, all these and others they anticipate and rehearse in their play hours. Upon us, who are further advanced and fairly dealing with the threads of destiny, they only glance from time to time to glean a hint for their own mimetic reproduction. Two children playing at soldiers are far more interesting to each other than one of the scarlet beings whom both are busy imitating. This is perhaps the greatest oddity of all. "Art for art"[15] is their motto; and the doings of grown folk are only interesting as the raw material for play. Not Théophile Gautier, not Flaubert,[16] can look more callously upon life, or rate the reproduction more highly over the reality; and they

14. Fictions.
15. The phrase "*l'art pour l'art*" was coined by French educational reformer and philosopher Victor Cousin (1792–1867) in the early nineteenth century.
16. Though very different stylistically, poet and literary critic Pierre Jules Théophile Gautier (1811–1872) and novelist Gustave Flaubert (1821–1880) viewed their work as a psychological antidote to the false world of the French middle class.

will parody an execution, a deathbed, or the funeral of the young man of Nain,[17] with all the cheerfulness in the world.

The true parallel for play is not to be found, of course, in conscious art, which, though it be derived from play, is itself an abstract, impersonal thing, and depends largely upon philosophical interests beyond the scope of childhood. It is when we make castles in the air and personate the leading character in our own romances, that we return to the spirit of our first years. Only, there are several reasons why the spirit is no longer so agreeable to indulge. Nowadays, when we admit this personal element into our divagations[18] we are apt to stir up uncomfortable and sorrowful memories, and remind ourselves sharply of old wounds. Our day-dreams can no longer lie all in the air like a story in the "Arabian Nights"; they read to us rather like the history of a period in which we ourselves had taken part, where we come across many unfortunate passages and find our own conduct smartly reprimanded. And then the child, mind you, acts his parts. He does not merely repeat them to himself; he leaps, he runs, and sets the blood agog over all his body. And so his play breathes him; and he no sooner assumes a passion than he gives it vent. Alas! when we betake ourselves to our intellectual form of play, sitting quietly by the fire or lying prone in bed, we rouse many hot feelings for which we can find no outlet. Substitutes are not acceptable to the mature mind, which desires the thing itself; and even to rehearse a triumphant dialogue with one's enemy, although it is perhaps the most satisfactory piece of play still left within our reach, is not entirely satisfying, and is even apt to lead to a visit and an interview which may be the reverse of triumphant after all.

In the child's world of dim sensation, play is all in all. "Making believe" is the gist of his whole life, and he cannot so much as take a walk except in character. I could not learn my alphabet

17. The young man of Nain is the first of three people Jesus raises from the dead (Luke 7:12–16).
18. Mental wanderings.

without some suitable *mise-en-scène*, and had to act a business man in an office before I could sit down to my book. Will you kindly question your memory, and find out how much you did, work or pleasure, in good faith and soberness, and for how much you had to cheat yourself with some invention? I remember, as though it were yesterday, the expansion of spirit, the dignity and self-reliance, that came with a pair of mustachios in burnt cork, even when there was none to see. Children are even content to forego what we call the realities, and prefer the shadow to the substance. When they might be speaking intelligibly together, they chatter senseless gibberish by the hour, and are quite happy because they are making believe to speak French. I have said already how even the imperious appetite of hunger suffers itself to be gulled and led by the nose with the fag end[19] of an old song. And it goes deeper than this: when children are together, even a meal is felt as an interruption in the business of life; and they must find some imaginative sanction, and tell themselves some sort of story, to account for, to colour, to render entertaining, the simple processes of eating and drinking. What wonderful fancies I have heard evolved out of the pattern upon tea-cups!—from which there followed a code of rules and a whole world of excitement, until tea-drinking began to take rank as a game. When my cousin and I took our porridge of a morning, we had a device to enliven the course of the meal. He ate his with sugar, and explained it to be a country continually buried under snow. I took mine with milk, and explained it to be a country suffering gradual inundation. You can imagine us exchanging bulletins; how here was an island still unsubmerged, here a valley not yet covered with snow; what inventions were made; how his population lived in cabins on perches and travelled on stilts, and how mine was always in boats; how the interest grew furious, as the last corner of safe ground was cut off on all sides and grew smaller every moment; and how, in fine, the

19. Remnant.

food was of altogether secondary importance, and might even have been nauseous, so long as we seasoned it with these dreams. But perhaps the most exciting moments I ever had over a meal were in the case of calves'-feet jelly. It was hardly possible not to believe—and you may be sure, so far from trying, I did all I could to favour the illusion—that some part of it was hollow, and that sooner or later my spoon would lay open the secret tabernacle of the golden rock. There, might some miniature *Red Beard*[20] await his hour; there, might one find the treasures of the *Forty Thieves*,[21] and bewildered Cassim beating about the walls. And so I quarried on slowly, with bated breath, savouring the interest. Believe me, I had little palate left for the jelly; and though I preferred the taste when I took cream with it, I used often to go without, because the cream dimmed the transparent fractures.

Even with games, this spirit is authoritative with right-minded children. It is thus that hide-and-seek has so pre-eminent a sovereignty, for it is the wellspring of romance, and the actions and the excitement to which it gives rise lend themselves to almost any sort of fable. And thus cricket, which is a mere matter of dexterity, palpably about nothing and for no end, often fails to satisfy infantile craving. It is a game, if you like, but not a game of play. You cannot tell yourself a story about cricket; and the activity it calls forth can be justified on no rational theory. Even football, although it admirably simulates the tug and the ebb and flow of battle, has presented difficulties to the mind of young sticklers after verisimilitude; and I knew at least one little boy who was mightily exercised about the presence of the ball, and had to spirit himself up, whenever he came to play, with an elaborate

---

20. According to medieval legend, the Holy Roman Emperor Frederick Barbarossa (1112–1190), or "Redbeard," as he was known, never died, but is hibernating in a hidden chamber inside the Untersberg, a mountain in the Bavarian Alps.

21. In "The Tale of Ali Baba and the Forty Thieves" in *The Arabian Nights*, Ali Baba discovers a treasure trove in a secret cave. His brother Kasim attempts to steal the treasure and becomes trapped in the cave.

story of enchantment, and take the missile as a sort of talisman bandied about in conflict between two Arabian nations.

To think of such a frame of mind is to become disquieted about the bringing up of children. Surely they dwell in a mythological epoch, and are not the contemporaries of their parents. What can they think of them? what can they make of these bearded or petticoated giants who look down upon their games? who move upon a cloudy Olympus, following unknown designs apart from rational enjoyment? who profess the tenderest solicitude for children, and yet every now and again reach down out of their altitude and terribly vindicate the prerogatives of age? Off goes the child, corporally smarting, but morally rebellious. Were there ever such unthinkable deities as parents? I would give a great deal to know what, in nine cases out of ten, is the child's unvarnished feeling. A sense of past cajolery; a sense of personal attraction, at best very feeble; above all, I should imagine, a sense of terror for the untried residue of mankind: go to make up the attraction that he feels. No wonder, poor little heart, with such a weltering[22] world in front of him, if he clings to the hand he knows! The dread irrationality of the whole affair, as it seems to children, is a thing we are all too ready to forget. "Oh, why," I remember passionately wondering, "why can we not all be happy and devote ourselves to play?" And when children do philosophize, I believe it is usually to very much the same purpose.

One thing, at least, comes very clearly out of these considerations; that whatever we are to expect at the hands of children, it should not be any peddling[23] exactitude about matters of fact. They walk in a vain show, and among mists and rainbows; they are passionate after dreams and unconcerned about realities; speech is a difficult art not wholly learned; and there is nothing in their own tastes or purposes to teach them what we mean by abstract

22. Turbulent.
23. Trifling.

truthfulness. When a bad writer is inexact, even if he can look back on half a century of years, we charge him with incompetence and not with dishonesty. And why not extend the same allowance to imperfect speakers? Let a stockbroker be dead stupid about poetry, or a poet inexact in the details of business, and we excuse them heartily from blame. But show us a miserable, unbreeched[24] human entity, whose whole profession it is to take a tub for a fortified town and a shaving-brush for the deadly stiletto, and who passes three-fourths of his time in a dream and the rest in open self-deception; and we expect him to be as nice upon a matter of fact as a scientific expert bearing evidence. Upon my heart, I think it less than decent. You do not consider how little the child sees, or how swift he is to weave what he has seen into bewildering fiction; and that he cares no more for what you call truth, than you for a gingerbread dragoon.[25]

I am reminded, as I write, that the child is very inquiring as to the precise truth of stories. But indeed this is a very different matter, and one bound up with the subject of play, and the precise amount of playfulness, or playability, to be looked for in the world. Many such burning questions must arise in the course of nursery education. Among the fauna of this planet, which already embraces the pretty soldier and the terrifying Irish beggarman, is, or is not, the child to expect a Bluebeard or a Cormoran?[26] Is he, or is he not, to look out for magicians, kindly and potent? May he, or may he not, reasonably hope to be cast away upon a desert island, or turned to such diminutive proportions that he can live on equal terms with his lead soldiery, and go a cruise in his own toy schooner? Surely all these are practical questions to a neophyte entering upon life with a view to play. Precision upon

---

24. Not yet wearing pants.
25. Soldier.
26. Bluebeard is a violent nobleman who stores the corpses of his murdered wives in a locked room. Cormoran is a giant who lives on a tidal island in Cornwall, England.

such a point, the child can understand. But if you merely ask him of his past behaviour, as to who threw such a stone, for instance, or struck such and such a match; or whether he had looked into a parcel or gone by a forbidden path,—why, he can see no moment in the inquiry, and it is ten to one, he has already half forgotten and half bemused himself with subsequent imaginings.

It would be easy to leave them in their native cloudland, where they figure so prettily—pretty like flowers and innocent like dogs. They will come out of their gardens soon enough, and have to go into offices and the witness-box. Spare them yet a while, O conscientious parent! Let them doze among their playthings yet a little! for who knows what a rough, war-faring existence lies before them in the future?

THE STIMULATION OF THE ALPS

To anyone who should come from a southern sanitarium to the Alps, the row of sunburned faces round the table would present the first surprise. He would begin by looking for the invalids, and he would lose his pains, for not one out of five of even the bad cases bears the mark of sickness on his face. The plump sunshine from above and its strong reverberation from below colour the skin like an Indian climate; the treatment, which consists mainly of the open air, exposes even the sickliest to tan, and a tableful of invalids comes, in a month or two, to resemble a tableful of hunters. But although he may be thus surprised at the first glance, his astonishment will grow greater as he experiences the effects of the climate on himself. In many ways it is a trying business to reside upon the Alps: the stomach is exercised, the appetite often languishes, the liver may at times rebel; and because you have come so far from metropolitan advantages, it does not follow that you shall recover. But one thing is undeniable—that in the rare air, clear, cold, and blinding light of Alpine winters, a man takes a certain troubled delight in his existence which can nowhere else be paralleled. He is perhaps no happier, but he is stingingly alive. It does not, perhaps, come out of him in work or exercise, yet he feels an enthusiasm of the blood unknown in more temperate climates. It may not be health, but it is fun.

There is nothing more difficult to communicate on paper than this baseless ardour, this stimulation of the brain, this sterile joyousness of spirits. You wake every morning, see the gold upon the snow-peaks, become filled with courage, and bless God for your prolonged existence. The valleys are but a stride to you; you cast your shoe over the hilltops; your ears and your heart sing; in the words of an unverified quotation from the Scots psalms, you feel yourself fit "on the wings of all the winds" to "come flying all abroad."[1] Europe and your mind are too narrow for that flood of energy. Yet it is notable that you are hard to root out of your bed; that you start forth singing, indeed, on your walk, yet are unusually ready to turn home again; that the best of you is volatile; and that although the restlessness remains till night, the strength is early at an end. With all these heady jollities, you are half conscious of an underlying languor in the body; you prove not to be so well as you had fancied; you weary before you have well begun; and though you mount at morning with the lark, that is not precisely a song-bird's heart that you bring back with you when you return with aching limbs and peevish temper to your inn.

It is hard to say wherein it lies, but this joy of Alpine winters is its own reward. Baseless, in a sense, it is more than worth more permanent improvements. The dream of health is perfect while it lasts; and if, in trying to realise it, you speedily wear out the dear hallucination, still every day, and many times a day, you are conscious of a strength you scarce possess, and a delight in living as merry as it proves to be transient.

1. The quoted text is from a metrical adaptation of Psalm 18 by Thomas Sternhold (1500–1549):

On cherubs and on cherubims
Full royally he road;
And on the wings of all the winds
Came flying all abroad.

It was published posthumously in 1561 in an expanded edition of his psalter of *The Book of Common Prayer*. Popular into the early eighteenth century, Sternhold's psalter was used throughout England and southern Scotland.

The brightness—heaven and earth conspiring to be bright—the levity and quiet of the air; the odd, stirring silence—more stirring than a tumult; the snow, the frost, the enchanted landscape: all have their part in the effect and on the memory, "*tous vous tapent sur la tête*";[2] and yet when you have enumerated all, you have gone no nearer to explain or even to qualify the delicate exhilaration that you feel—delicate, you may say, and yet excessive, greater than can be said in prose, almost greater than an invalid can bear. There is a certain wine of France,[3] known in England in some gaseous disguise, but when drunk in the land of its nativity still as a pool, clean as river water, and as heady as verse. It is more than probable that in its noble natural condition this was the very wine of Anjou so beloved by Athos in the "Musketeers."[4] Now, if the reader has ever washed down a liberal second breakfast with the wine in question, and gone forth, on the back of these dilutions, into a sultry, sparkling noontide, he will have felt an influence almost as genial, although strangely grosser, than this fairy titillation of the nerves among the snow and sunshine of the Alps. That also is a mode, we need not say of intoxication, but of insobriety. Thus also a man walks in a strong sunshine of the mind, and follows smiling, insubstantial meditations. And whether he be really so clever or so strong as he supposes, in either case he will enjoy his chimera while it lasts.

The influence of this giddy air displays itself in many secondary ways. A certain sort of laboured pleasantry has already been recognised, and may perhaps have been remarked in these papers, as a sort peculiar to that climate. People utter their judgments with a cannonade of syllables; a big word is as good as a meal to them; and the turn of a phrase goes further than humour or wisdom. By the professional writer many sad vicissitudes have to be undergone. At first, he cannot write at all. The heart, it appears,

2. "It all hits you over the head."
3. Coteaux Champenois, or Champagne without the bubbles.
4. Athos is one of the three musketeers in Alexandre Dumas's 1844 novel.

is unequal to the pressure of business, and the brain, left without nourishment, goes into a mild decline. Next, some power of work returns to him, accompanied by jumping headaches. Last, the spring is opened, and there pours at once from his pen a world of blatant, hustling polysyllables, and talk so high as, in the old joke, to be positively offensive in hot weather. He writes it in good faith and with a sense of inspiration; it is only when he comes to read what he has written that surprise and disquiet seize upon his mind. What is he to do, poor man? All his little fishes talk like whales. This yeasty inflation, this stiff and strutting architecture of the sentence, has come upon him while he slept; and it is not he, it is the Alps that are to blame. He is not, perhaps, alone, which somewhat comforts him. Nor is the ill without a remedy. Someday, when the spring returns, he shall go down a little lower in this world, and remember quieter inflections and more modest language. But here, in the meantime, there seems to swim up some outline of a new cerebral hygiene and a good time coming, when experienced advisers shall send a man to the proper measured level for the ode, the biography, the religious tract; and a nook may be found, between the sea and Chimborazo,[5] where Mr. Swinburne[6] shall be able to write more continently, and Mr. Browning[7] somewhat slower.

Is it a return of youth, or is it a congestion of the brain? It is a sort of congestion, perhaps, that leads the invalid, when all goes well, to face the new day with such a bubbling cheerfulness. It is certainly congestion that makes night hideous with visions, all the chambers of a many-storied caravanserai[8] haunted with vociferous nightmares, and many wakeful people come down late for breakfast in the morning. Upon that theory the cynic may explain

5. A mountain in Ecuador.

6. Algernon Charles Swinburne (1837–1909), English poet known for his florid style and overt eroticism.

7. Robert Browning (1812–1889), English poet known for his enigmatic and intricate dramatic monologues.

8. A roadside inn, originally along trade routes.

the whole affair—exhilaration, nightmares, pomp of tongue and all. But, on the other hand, the peculiar blessedness of boyhood may itself be but a symptom of the same complaint, for the two effects are strangely similar; and the frame of mind of the invalid upon the Alps is a sort of intermittent youth, with periods of lassitude. The fountain of Juventus[9] does not play steadily in these parts; but there it plays, and possibly nowhere else.

9. The Roman god of youth.

NURSES

I knew one once,[1] and the room where, lonely and old, she waited for death. It was pleasant enough, high up above the lane, and looking forth upon a hill-side, covered all day with sheets and yellow blankets, and with long lines of underclothing fluttering between the battered posts. There were any number of cheap prints, and a drawing by one of "her children," and there were flowers in the window, and a sickly canary withered into consumption in an ornamental cage. The bed, with its checked coverlid, was in a closet.[2] A great Bible lay on the table; and her drawers were full of "scones," which it was her pleasure to give to young visitors such as I was then.

You may not think this a melancholy picture; but the canary, and the cat, and the white mouse that she had for a while, and that died, were all indications of the want that ate into her heart.

1. With his plaintive "I knew one once," Stevenson echoes Hamlet in the graveyard: "Alas, poor Yorick! I knew him, Horatio, a fellow of infinite jest, of most excellent fancy. He hath borne me on his back a thousand times" (5.1.185–88). The brokenhearted nurse in this character study stands in sharp contrast to Stevenson's own childhood nurse: his beloved Alison "Cummy" Cunningham (1822–1913), with whom he corresponded regularly throughout his life. He dedicated *A Child's Garden of Verses* to Cunningham, said of her, she was "My second Mother, my first Wife, / The angel of my infant life." Even so, Stevenson's guilt is palpable. Like many women in her profession, Cunningham sacrificed a lot. She turned away suitors, choosing her job over having children of her own.
2. Alcove.

I think I know a little of what that old woman felt; and I am as sure as if I had seen her, that she sat many an hour in silent tears, with the big Bible open before her clouded eyes.

If you could look back upon her life, and feel the great chain that had linked her to one child after another, sometimes to be wrenched suddenly through, and sometimes, which is infinitely worse, to be torn gradually off through years of growing neglect, or perhaps growing dislike! She had, like the mother, overcome that natural repugnance—repugnance which no man can conquer—towards the infirm and helpless mass of putty of the earlier stage. She had spent her best and happiest years in tending, watching, and learning to love like a mother this child, with which she has no connection and to which she has no tie. Perhaps she refused some sweetheart (such things have been), or put him off and off, until he lost heart and turned to someone else, all for fear of leaving this creature that had wound itself about her heart. And the end of it all—her month's warning, and a present perhaps, and the rest of the life to vain regret. Or, worse still, to see the child gradually forgetting and forsaking her, fostered in disrespect and neglect on the plea of growing manliness, and at last beginning to treat her as a servant whom he had treated a few years before as a mother. She sees the Bible or the Psalm-book, which with gladness and love unutterable in her heart she had bought for him years ago out of her slender savings, neglected for some newer gift of his father, lying in dust in the lumber-room[3] or given away to a poor child, and the act applauded for its unfeeling charity. Little wonder if she becomes hurt and angry, and attempts to tyrannise and to grasp her old power back again. We are not all patient Grizzels,[4] by good fortune, but the most of us human beings with feelings and tempers of our own.

3. A storage room for furniture.
4. Grizzel Clay is a sweet-tempered dairymaid in "Going to the Mop" (1871) by English novelist Ellen Wood (1814–1887). Wood's story—part of her popular "Johnny Ludlow" series—first appeared in her literary journal *The Argosy*.

And so in the end, behold her in the room that I described. Very likely and very naturally, in some fling of feverish misery or recoil of thwarted love, she has quarrelled with her old employers and the children are forbidden to see her or to speak to her; or at best she gets her rent paid and a little to herself, and now and then her late charges are sent up (with another nurse, perhaps) to pay her a short visit. How bright these visits seem as she looks forward to them on her lonely bed! How unsatisfactory their realisation, when the forgetful child, half wondering, checks with every word and action the outpouring of her maternal love! How bitter and restless the memories that they leave behind. And for the rest, what else has she?—to watch them with eager eyes as they go to school, to sit in church where she can see them every Sunday, to be passed someday unnoticed in the street, or deliberately cut because the great man or the great woman are with friends before whom they are ashamed to recognise the old woman that loved them.

When she goes home that night, how lonely will the room appear to her! Perhaps the neighbours may hear her sobbing to herself in the dark, with the fire burnt out for want of fuel, and the candle still unlit upon the table.

And it is for this that they live, these quasi-mothers—mothers in everything but the travail and the thanks. It is for this that they have remained virtuous in youth, living the dull life of a household servant. It is for this that they refused the old sweetheart, and have no fireside or offspring of their own.

I believe in a better state of things, that there will be no more nurses, and that every mother will nurse her own offspring; for what can be more hardening and demoralising than to call forth the tenderest feelings of a woman's heart and cherish them yourself as long as you need them, as long as your children require a nurse to love them, and then to blight and thwart and destroy them, whenever your own use for them is at an end. This may be Utopian; but it is always a little thing if one mother or two mothers can be brought to feel more tenderly to those who share their toil and have no part in their reward.

SAN FRANCISCO

The Pacific coast of the United States, as you may see by the map, and still better in that admirable book, "Two Years Before the Mast," by Dana,[1] is one of the most exposed and shelterless on earth. The trade-wind blows fresh; the huge Pacific swell booms along degree after degree of an unbroken line of coast. South of the joint firth[2] of the Columbia and Williamette,[3] there flows in no considerable river; south of Puget Sound there is no protected inlet of the ocean. Along the whole seaboard of California there are but two unexceptionable[4] anchorages, the bight[5] of the Bay of Monterey, and the inland sea that takes its name from San Francisco.

Whether or not it was here that Drake[6] put in in 1597,[7] we cannot tell. There is no other place so suitable; and yet the narrative of Francis Pretty[8] scarcely seems to suit the features of

1. Richard Henry Dana Jr. (1815–1882), American statesman and writer.
2. A Scots catch-all for "estuary," "inlet," "fjord," and "strait."
3. Willamette River in Oregon.
4. Indisputable.
5. Curved coastline.
6. Francis Drake (c.1540–1596), sea captain and privateer.
7. Stevenson means 1579.
8. A gentleman-soldier who accompanied Drake, Pretty penned an account of their expedition, *Sir Francis Drake's Famous Voyage Round the World* (1580), which included a brief description of the "fair and good bay."

the scene. Viewed from seaward, the Golden Gates[9] should give no very English impression to justify the name of a New Albion.[10] On the west, the deep lies open; nothing near but the still vexed Farallones.[11] The coast is rough and barren. Tamalpais, a mountain of a memorable figure, springing direct from the sea-level, over-plumbs the narrow entrance from the north. On the south, the loud music of the Pacific sounds along beaches and cliffs, and among broken reefs, the sporting-place of the sea-lion. Dismal, shifting sand hills, wrinkled by the wind, appear behind. Perhaps, too, in the days of Drake, Tamalpais would be clothed to its peak with the majestic redwoods.

Within the memory of persons not yet old, a mariner might have steered into these narrows—not yet the Golden Gates—opened out the surface of the bay—here girt with hills, there lying broad to the horizon—and beheld a scene as empty of the presence, as pure from the handiwork, of man, as in the days of our old sea-commander. A Spanish mission, fort, and church[12] took the place of those "houses of the people of the country"[13] which were seen by Pretty, "close to the water-side." All else would be unchanged. Now, a generation later, a great city covers the sand-hills on the west, a growing town lies along the muddy shallows of the east; steamboats pant continually between them from before sunrise till the small hours of the morning; lines of great sea-going ships lie ranged at anchor; colours fly upon the islands; and from all around the hum of corporate life, of beaten bells, and steam, and

9. Here, and throughout his California writings, Stevenson refers to the Golden Gate as the "Golden Gates."

10. "Albion" is an ancient name for the island of Great Britain, a reference, some believe, to the white cliffs of Dover. Drake named North America "New Albion."

11. A group of rocky, windswept islands thirty miles west of San Francisco.

12. Mission Dolores and the Presidio were established by the Spanish in 1776.

13. Pretty gives the following account of the homes of the indigenous population: "Their houses are digged round about with earth, and have from the uttermost brims of the circle, clifts of wood set upon them, joining close together at the top like a spire steeple, which by reason of that closeness are very warm. Their bed is the ground with rushes strowed on it; and lying about the house, [they] have the fire in the midst."

running carriages, goes cheerily abroad in the sunshine. Choose a place on one of the huge, throbbing ferry-boats, and, when you are midway between the city and the suburb, look around. The air is fresh and salt as if you were at sea. On the one hand is Oakland, gleaming white among its gardens. On the other, to seaward, hill after hill is crowded and crowned with the palaces of San Francisco; its long streets lie in regular bars of darkness, east and west, across the sparkling picture; a forest of masts bristles like bulrushes about its feet; nothing remains of the days of Drake but the faithful trade-wind scattering the smoke, the fogs that will begin to muster about sundown, and the fine bulk of Tamalpais looking down on San Francisco, like Arthur's Seat[14] on Edinburgh.

Thus, in the course of a generation only, this city and its suburb have arisen. Men are alive by the score who have hunted all over the foundations in a dreary waste. I have dined, near the "punctual centre"[15] of San Francisco, with a gentleman (then newly married) who told me of his former pleasures, wading with his fowling-piece in sand and scrub, on the site of the house where we were dining. In this busy, moving generation, we have all known cities to cover our boyish playgrounds, we have all started for a country walk and stumbled on a new suburb; but I wonder what enchantment of the Arabian Nights can have equalled this evocation of a roaring city, in a few years of a man's life, from the marshes and the blowing sand. Such swiftness of increase, as with an overgrown youth, suggests a corresponding swiftness of destruction. The sandy peninsula of San Francisco, mirroring itself on one side in the bay, beaten, on the other, by the surge of the Pacific, and shaken to the heart by frequent earthquakes, seems in itself no very durable foundation. According to Indian tales, perhaps older than the name of California, it once rose out of the sea in a moment, and some time or other shall, in a moment, sink again. No Indian, they say, cares to linger on that doubtful land.

14. A hill overlooking Edinburgh.
15. Near the Stock Exchange with its large clock.

"The earth hath bubbles as the water has, and this is of them."[16] Here, indeed all is new, nature as well as towns. The very hills of California have an unfinished look; the rains and the streams have not yet carved them to their perfect shape. The forests spring like mushrooms from the unexhausted soil; and they are mown down yearly by forest fires. We are in early geological epochs, changeful and insecure; and we feel, as with a sculptor's model,[17] that the author may yet grow weary of and shatter the rough sketch.

Fancy apart, San Francisco is a city beleaguered with alarms. The lower parts, along the bay side, sit on piles:[18] old wrecks decaying, fish dwelling unsunned, beneath the populous houses; and a trifling subsidence[19] might drown the business quarters in an hour. Earthquakes are not only common, they are sometimes threatening in their violence; the fear of them grows yearly on a resident; he begins with indifference, ends in sheer panic; and no one feels safe in any but a wooden house. Hence it comes that, in that rainless clime, the whole city is built of timber—a woodyard of unusual extent and complication; that fires spring up readily, and, served by the unwearying trade-wind, swiftly spread; that all over the city there are fire-signal boxes; that the sound of the bell, telling the number of the threatened ward, is soon familiar to the ear; and that nowhere else in the world is the art of the fireman carried to so nice a point.

Next, perhaps, in order of strangeness to the rapidity of its appearance, is the mingling of the races that combine to people it. The town is essentially not Anglo-Saxon; still more essentially not American. The Yankee and the Englishman find themselves alike in a strange country. There are none of those touches—not of nature, and I dare scarcely say of art—by which the Anglo-Saxon

16. From Shakespeare's *Macbeth*: "The earth hath bubbles as the water has, / And these are of them" (1.3.79–80).
17. A small clay or wax model of a proposed sculpture.
18. Wooden posts driven into the ground to support a structure, in this case a makeshift amalgamation of landfill and wharves.
19. Cave-in.

feels himself at home in so great a diversity of lands. Here, on the contrary, are airs of Marseilles and of Pekin.[20] The shops along the street are like the consulates of different nations. The passers-by vary in feature like the slides of a magic-lantern.[21] For we are here in that city of gold to which adventurers congregated out of all the winds of heaven;[22] we are in a land that till the other day was ruled and peopled by the countrymen of Cortés;[23] and the sea that laves the piers of San Francisco is the ocean of the East and of the isles of summer. There goes the Mexican, unmistakable; there the blue-clad Chinaman with his white slippers; there the soft-spoken, brown Kanaka,[24] or perhaps a waif from far-away Malaya.[25] You hear French, German, Italian, Spanish, and English indifferently. You taste the food of all nations in the various restaurants; passing from a French *prix-fixe*,[26] where everyone is French, to a roaring German ordinary[27] where everyone is German; ending, perhaps, in a cool and silent Chinese tea-house. For every man, for every race and nation, that city is a foreign city; humming with foreign tongues and customs; and yet each and all have made themselves at home. The Germans have a German theatre and innumerable beer-gardens. The French Fall of the Bastille[28] is celebrated with squibs[29] and banners, and marching patriots, as noisily as the

---

20. Peking; modern-day Beijing.
21. An apparatus that projects images on a wall or screen.
22. From *Hamlet*:

> So excellent a king, that was to this
> Hyperion to a satyr, so loving to my mother
> That he might not beteem the winds of heaven
> Visit her face too roughly. (1.2.139–42)

23. Hernán Cortés (1485–1547), Spanish Conquistador.
24. Hawaiian.
25. Malaysia.
26. A restaurant that serves a multicourse meal at a fixed price.
27. British term for a *prix-fixe* restaurant.
28. The Fourteenth of July is France's *la Fête nationale* (National Celebration). It commemorates the storming of the Bastille Prison in 1789 during the French Revolution.
29. Fireworks.

American Fourth of July. The Italians have their dear domestic quarter, with Italian caricatures in the windows, Chianti and polenta in the taverns. The Chinese are settled as in China. The goods they offer for sale are as foreign as the lettering on the signboard of the shop: dried fish from the China seas; pale cakes and sweetmeats—the like, perhaps, once eaten by Badroubadour;[30] nuts of unfriendly[31] shape; ambiguous, outlandish vegetables, misshapen, lean or bulbous—telling of a country where the trees are not as our trees, and the very back garden is a cabinet of curiosities. The joss-house[32] is hard by, heavy with incense, packed with quaint carvings and the paraphernalia of a foreign ceremonial. All these you behold, crowded together in the narrower arteries of the city, cool, sunless, a little mouldy, with the high, musical sing-song of that alien language in your ears. Yet the houses are of Occidental build: the lines of a hundred telegraphs pass, thick as a ship's rigging, overhead, a kite hanging among them perhaps, or perhaps two, one European, one Chinese in shape and colour; mercantile Jack,[33] the Italian fisher, the Dutch merchant, the Mexican vaquero[34] go hustling by; at the sunny end of the street, a thoroughfare roars with European traffic; and meanwhile, high and clear, out breaks perhaps the San Francisco fire-alarm, and people pause to count the strokes, and in the stations of the double fire-service you know that the electric bells are ringing, the traps opening, and clapping to, and the engine, manned and harnessed, being whisked into the street, before the sound of the alarm has ceased to vibrate on your ear. Of all romantic places for a boy to loiter in, that Chinese quarter is the most romantic. There, on a half-holiday,[35] three doors from home, he may visit an actual

30. Badroulbadour is the Chinese princess who marries Aladdin in "The Story of Aladdin, or The Magic Lamp" in *The Arabian Nights*.
31. Off-putting.
32. Chinese temple or shrine.
33. Sailor.
34. Cowboy.
35. A day when school lets out early.

foreign land, foreign in people, language, things, and customs. The very barber of the Arabian Nights[36] shall be at work before him, shaving heads; he shall see Aladdin playing on the streets; who knows, but among those nameless vegetables, the fruit of the nose-tree[37] itself may be exposed for sale? And the interest is heightened with a chill of horror. Below, you hear, the cellars are alive with mystery; opium dens, where the smokers lie one above another, shelf above shelf, close-packed and grovelling in deadly stupor; the seats of unknown vices and cruelties, the prisons of unacknowledged slaves and the secret lazarettos[38] of disease.

With all this mass of nationalities, crime is common. [Amid such a competition of respectabilities, the moral sense is confused; in this camp of gold-seekers, speech is loud and the hand is ready.][39] There are rough quarters where it is dangerous o' nights; cellars of public entertainment which the wary pleasure-seeker chooses to avoid. Concealed weapons are unlawful, but the law is continually broken. One editor was shot dead while I was there; another walked the streets accompanied by a bravo,[40] his guardian angel. I have been quietly eating a dish of oysters in a restaurant, where, not more than ten minutes after I had left, shots were exchanged and took effect; and one night about ten o'clock, I saw a man standing watchfully at a street-corner with a long Smith-and-Wesson glittering in his hand behind his back. Somebody had done something he should not, and was being looked for with a vengeance. It is odd, too, that the seat of the last vigilance

---

36. The Barber of Baghdad.
37. "The Nose-Tree" is an old German folktale about a magic apple tree. When eaten, the apples cause the eater's nose to grow until it drags on the ground. Only the fruit of a magic pear tree can restore the nose to its original state.
38. Quarantine stations.
39. Stevenson later omitted this sentence, worried it would offend American readers.
40. Bodyguard.

committee[41] I know of—a mediæval *Vehmgericht*[42]—was none other than the Palace Hotel,[43] the world's greatest caravanserai,[44] served by lifts and lit with electricity; where, in the great glazed court, a band nightly discourses music from a grove of palms. So do extremes meet in this city of contrasts: extremes of wealth and poverty, apathy and excitement, the conveniences of civilisation and the red justice of Judge Lynch.[45]

The streets lie straight up and down the hills, and straight across at right angles, these in sun, those in shadow, a trenchant pattern of gloom and glare; and what with the crisp illumination, the sea-air singing in your ears, the chill and glitter, the changing aspects both of things and people, the fresh sights at every corner of your walk—sights of the bay, of Tamalpais, of steep, descending streets, of the outspread city—whiffs of alien speech, sailors singing on shipboard, Chinese coolies[46] toiling on the shore, crowds brawling all day in the street before the Stock Exchange—one brief impression follows and obliterates another, and the city leaves upon the mind no general and stable picture, but a profusion of airy and incongruous images, of the sea and shore, the east and west, the summer and the winter.

In the better parts of this most interesting city there is apt to be a touch of the commonplace. It is in the slums and suburbs that the city dilettante finds his game. And there is nothing more characteristic and original than the outlying quarters of San Francisco. The Chinese district is the most famous; but it is

41. A body of vigilantes.
42. In response to chaos created by feudal warfare, civic leaders in twelfth-century Westphalia established Vehmic courts, extralegal and highly secretive criminal tribunals. Walter Scott discusses the *Vehmgericht* in his historical novel *Anne of Geierstein* (1829).
43. A luxury hotel on Montgomery Street in the old Financial District of San Francisco.
44. An inn on a caravan route.
45. Charles Lynch (1736–1796) was a Virginia farmer, politician and justice of the peace who created an extralegal court to punish British loyalists. The word "lynching" is his legacy.
46. In the lingo of empire, a "coolie" is an unskilled Asian laborer.

far from the only truffle in the pie. There is many another dingy corner, many a young antiquity, many a *terrain vague*[47] with that stamp of quaintness that the city lover seeks and dwells on; and the indefinite prolongation of its streets, up hill and down dale, makes San Francisco a place apart. The same street in its career visits and unites so many different classes of society, here echoing with drays,[48] there lying decorously silent between the mansions of Bonanza[49] millionaires, to founder at last among the drifting sands beside Lone Mountain cemetery,[50] or die out among the sheds and lumber of the north. Thus you may be struck with a spot, set it down for the most romantic in the city, and, glancing at the name-plate, find it is on the same street that you yourself inhabit in another quarter of the town.

The great net of straight thoroughfares lying at right angles, east and west and north and south, over the shoulders of Nob Hill, the hill of palaces, must certainly be counted the best part of San Francisco. It is there that the millionaires are gathered together vying with each other in display. From thence, looking down over the business wards of the city, we can descry a building with a little belfry, and that is the Stock Exchange, the heart of San Francisco: a great pump we might call it, continually pumping up the savings of the lower quarters into the pockets of the millionaires upon the hill. But these same thoroughfares that enjoy for awhile so elegant a destiny have their lines prolonged into more unpleasant places. Some meet their fate in the sands; some must take a cruise in the ill-famed[51] China quarters; some run into the sea; some perish unwept among pig-sties and rubbish-heaps.

47. *Terrain vague* means "waste ground" or "vacant lot." Stevenson uses the term to suggest a gap in expectation or an anomaly in a cityscape.
48. Wagons for transporting goods.
49. In mining, a "bonanza" is a large deposit of mineral. A "Bonanza millionaire" is a goldminer who struck it rich during the California Gold Rush (1848–55).
50. Lone Mountain is a hill in the center of modern-day San Francisco. In the 1870s, it was the location of a cemetery. The hill marked the western extent of residential San Francisco. Beyond it, sand dunes and scrub stretched to the ocean.
51. Infamous.

Nob Hill comes, of right, in the place of honour; but the two other hills of San Francisco are more entertaining to explore. On both there are a world of old wooden houses snoozing together all forgotten. Some are of the quaintest design, others only romantic by neglect and age. Some have been almost undermined by new thoroughfares, and sit high up on the margin of the sandy cutting, only to be reached by stairs. Some are curiously painted, and I have seen one at least with ancient carvings panelled in its wall. Surely they are not of Californian building, but far voyagers from round the stormy Horn,[52] like those who sent for them and dwelt in them at first. Brought to be the favourites of the wealthy, they have sunk into these poor, forgotten districts, where, like old town toasts,[53] they keep each other silently in countenance. Telegraph Hill and Rincon Hill, these are the dozing quarters that I recommend to the city dilettante. There stand these forgotten houses, enjoying the unbroken sun and quiet. There, if there were such an author, would the San Francisco Fortuné de Boisgobey[54] pitch the first chapter of his mystery. But the first is the quainter of the two, and commands, moreover, a noble view. As it stands at the turn of the bay, its skirts are all waterside, and round from North Reach[55] to the Bay Front you can follow doubtful paths from one quaint corner to another. Everywhere the same tumble-down decay and sloppy progress, new things yet unmade, old things tottering to their fall; everywhere the same out-at-elbows,[56] many-nationed loungers at dim, irregular grog-shops;[57] everywhere the same sea-air and isleted sea-prospect; and for a last and more romantic note, you have on the one hand Tamalpais standing high in the blue air, and on the other the tail of that long alignment of

52. Cape Horn.
53. Tipplers.
54. Fortuné du Boisgobey was the *nom de plume* of the popular French crime novelist Fortuné Hippolyte Auguste Abraham-Dubois (1821–1891).
55. Stevenson means North Beach.
56. Shabbily dressed.
57. Bars.

three-masted, full-rigged, deep-sea ships that make a forest of spars along the eastern front of San Francisco. In no other port is such a navy congregated. For the coast trade is so trifling, and the ocean trade from round the Horn so large, that the smaller ships are swallowed up, and can do nothing to confuse the majestic order of these merchant princes. In an age when the ship-of-the-line[58] is already a thing of the past, and we can never again hope to go coasting in a cock-boat[59] between the "wooden walls" of a squadron at anchor, there is perhaps no place on earth where the power and beauty of sea architecture can be so perfectly enjoyed as in this bay.

58. Massive warships deployed in the first line of battle.
59. A small boat used to service large ships.

NUITS BLANCHES

If anyone should know the pleasure and pain of a sleepless night, it should be I.[1] I remember, so long ago, the sickly child that woke from his few hours' slumber with the sweat of a nightmare on his brow, to lie awake and listen and long for the first signs of life among the silent streets. These nights of pain and weariness are graven on my mind; and so when the same thing happened to me again, everything that I heard or saw was rather a recollection than a discovery.

Weighed upon by the opaque and almost sensible darkness, I listened eagerly for anything to break the sepulchral quiet. But nothing came, save, perhaps, an emphatic crack from the old cabinet that was made by Deacon Brodie,[2] or the dry rustle of the coals on the extinguished fire. It was a calm; or I know that I should have heard in the roar and clatter of the storm, as I have not heard it for so many years, the wild career[3] of a horseman, always scouring up from the distance and passing swiftly below the window; yet always returning again from the place whence first he came, as

1. *Nuit blanche* means "sleepless night" in French.
2. William Brodie (1741–1788) was a prosperous cabinet-maker and Edinburgh city councilor, who was arrested, tried and hanged when it was discovered he was also a burglar. In 1869, Stevenson wrote a melodrama about the scandal, *Deacon Brodie, or The Double Life*.
3. Gallop.

though, baffled by some higher power, he had retraced his steps to gain impetus for another and another attempt.

As I lay there, there arose out of the utter stillness the rumbling of a carriage a very great way off, that drew near, and passed within a few streets of the house, and died away as gradually as it had arisen. This, too, was as a reminiscence.

I rose and lifted a corner of the blind. Over the black belt of the garden I saw the long line of Queen Street,[4] with here and there a lighted window. How often before had my nurse[5] lifted me out of bed and pointed them out to me, while we wondered together if, there also, there were children that could not sleep, and if these lighted oblongs were signs of those that waited like us for the morning.

I went out into the lobby, and looked down into the great deep well of the staircase. For what cause I know not, just as it used to be in the old days that the feverish child might be the better served, a peep of gas illuminated a narrow circle far below me. But where I was, all was darkness and silence, save the dry monotonous ticking of the clock that came ceaselessly up to my ear.

The final crown of it all, however, the last touch of reproduction on the pictures of my memory, was the arrival of that time for which, all night through, I waited and longed of old. It was my custom, as the hours dragged on, to repeat the question, "When will the carts come in?" and repeat it again and again until at last those sounds arose in the street that I have heard once more this morning. The road before our house is a great thoroughfare for early carts. I know not, and I never have known, what they carry, whence they come, or whither they go. But I know that, long ere dawn, and for hours together, they stream continuously past, with the same rolling and jerking of wheels and the same clink of horses' feet. It was not for nothing that they made the burthen of

4. When Stevenson was six, his family moved to Heriot Row in Edinburgh, across the street from the Queen Street Gardens.

5. See "Nurses."

my wishes all night through. They are really the first throbbings of life, the harbingers of day; and it pleases you as much to hear them as it must please a shipwrecked seaman once again to grasp a hand of flesh and blood after years of miserable solitude. They have the freshness of the daylight life about them. You can hear the carters cracking their whips and crying hoarsely to their horses or to one another; and sometimes even a peal of healthy, harsh horse-laughter comes up to you through the darkness. There is now an end of mystery and fear. Like the knocking at the door in *Macbeth,*[6] or the cry of the watchman in the *Tour de Nesle,*[7] they show that the horrible cæsura[8] is over and the nightmares have fled away, because the day is breaking and the ordinary life of men is beginning to bestir itself among the streets.

In the middle of it all I fell asleep, to be wakened by the officious knocking at my door, and I find myself twelve years older than I had dreamed myself all night.

---

6. See a short essay of De Quincey's. [*Stevenson*]

At one point in *Macbeth*, the sound of knocking interrupts a conversation between conspirators Macbeth and Lady Macbeth: "Whence is that knocking? / How Is 't with me, when every noise appalls me?" (2.2.56-57). In "On the Knocking at the Gate in *Macbeth*" (1823), English essayist Thomas de Quincey (1785–1859) analyzes why the audience, too, is so unnerved by the knocking, when we should be rooting against Macbeth. It is because, unconsciously, we find it less painful to identify with a murderer than with a victim. In unwittingly transferring our sympathies to Macbeth, we distance ourselves from the unbearable horror of death.

7. Written by Alexandre Dumas and Frédéric Gaillardet, *La Tour de Nesle* (1832) is a historical play about a royal adultery scandal in fourteenth-century France.

8. Interlude.

ON THE ENJOYMENT OF UNPLEASANT PLACES

It is a difficult matter to make the most of any given place, and we have much in our own power. Things looked at patiently from one side after another generally end by showing a side that is beautiful. A few months ago some words were said in the *Portfolio*[1] as to an "austere regimen in scenery"; and such a discipline was then recommended as "healthful and strengthening to the taste." That is the text, so to speak, of the present essay. This discipline in scenery, it must be understood, is something more than a mere walk before breakfast to whet the appetite. For when we are put down in some unsightly neighbourhood, and especially if we have come to be more or less dependent on what we see, we must set ourselves to hunt out beautiful things with all the ardour and patience of a botanist after a rare plant. Day by day we perfect ourselves in the art of seeing nature more favourably. We learn to live with her, as people learn to live with fretful or violent spouses: to dwell lovingly on what is good, and shut our eyes against all that is bleak or inharmonious. We learn, also, to come to each place in the right spirit. The traveller, as Brantôme[2]

1. The literary magazine *Portfolio* was founded in 1869 by art critic Philip Gilbert Hamerton (1834–1894), who published several of Stevenson's essays, including "On the Enjoyment of Unpleasant Places."
2. Pierre de Bourdeille, Abbé de Brantôme (c.1540–1614), French historian, cleric and soldier.

quaintly tells us, *"fait des discours en soi pour se soutenir en chemin"*;[3] and into these discourses he weaves something out of all that he sees and suffers by the way; they take their tone greatly from the varying character of the scene; a sharp ascent brings different thoughts from a level road; and the man's fancies grow lighter as he comes out of the wood into a clearing. Nor does the scenery any more affect the thoughts than the thoughts affect the scenery. We see places through our humours as through differently-coloured glasses. We are ourselves a term in the equation, a note of the chord, and make discord or harmony almost at will. There is no fear for the result, if we can but surrender ourselves sufficiently to the country that surrounds and follows us, so that we are ever thinking suitable thoughts or telling ourselves some suitable sort of story as we go. We become thus, in some sense, a centre of beauty; we are provocative of beauty, much as a gentle and sincere character is provocative of sincerity and gentleness in others. And even where there is no harmony to be elicited by the quickest and most obedient of spirits, we may still embellish a place with some attraction of romance. We may learn to go far afield for associations, and handle them lightly when we have found them. Sometimes an old print comes to our aid; I have seen many a spot lit up at once with picturesque imaginations, by a reminiscence of Callot, or Sadeler, or Paul Brill.[4] Dick Turpin[5] has been my lay figure for many an English lane. And I suppose the Trossachs[6] would hardly be the Trossachs for most tourists if a man of admirable romantic instinct had not peopled it for them with harmonious figures, and brought them thither with minds rightly prepared for the impression. There is half the battle in this preparation. For instance: I have rarely been able to visit, in the proper

3. "talks to himself to lift his spirits on the road"
4. Jacques Callot (c.1592–1632), printmaker from Lorraine; Aegidius Sadeler (1570–1629), Flemish engraver; Paul Bril (1554–1626), Flemish landscape painter.
5. Richard Turpin (c.1705–1739), notorious English highwayman.
6. Walter Scott's poem *The Lady of the Lake* (1810) is set in the Trossachs, a picturesque wooded valley in central Scotland.

spirit, the wild and inhospitable places of our own Highlands. I am happier where it is tame and fertile, and not readily pleased without trees. I understand that there are some phases of mental trouble that harmonise well with such surroundings, and that some persons, by the dispensing power of the imagination, can go back several centuries in spirit, and put themselves into sympathy with the hunted, houseless, unsociable way of life that was in its place upon these savage hills. Now, when I am sad, I like nature to charm me out of my sadness, like David before Saul;[7] and the thought of these past ages strikes nothing in me but an unpleasant pity; so that I can never hit on the right humour for this sort of landscape, and lose much pleasure in consequence. Still, even here, if I were only let alone, and time enough were given, I should have all manner of pleasures, and take many clear and beautiful images away with me when I left. When we cannot think ourselves into sympathy with the great features of a country, we learn to ignore them, and put our head among the grass for flowers, or pore, for long times together, over the changeful current of a stream. We come down to the sermon in stones,[8] when we are shut out from any poem in the spread landscape. We begin to peep and botanise, we take an interest in birds and insects, we find many things beautiful in miniature. The reader will recollect the little summer scene in "Wuthering Heights"[9]—the one warm scene, perhaps, in all that powerful, miserable novel—and the great feature that is made therein by grasses and flowers and a little sunshine: this is in the spirit of which I now speak. And, lastly,

---

7. When Saul is stricken with sadness, only David's harp can lift his spirits. "And it came to pass, when the *evil* spirit from God was upon Saul, that David took an harp, and played with his hands; so Saul was refreshed, and was well, and the evil spirit departed from him" (I Samuel 16:23).

8. From Shakespeare's *As You Like It* (c.1599):

> And this our life, exempt from public haunt,
> Finds tongues in trees, books in the running brooks,
> Sermons in stones, and good in everything. (2.1.15–17)

9. The scene in *Wuthering Heights* (1847) is in Chapter 24.

we can go indoors; interiors are sometimes as beautiful, often more picturesque, than the shows of the open air, and they have that quality of shelter of which I shall presently have more to say.

With all this in mind, I have often been tempted to put forth the paradox that any place is good enough to live a life in, while it is only in a few, and those highly favoured, that we can pass a few hours agreeably. For, if we only stay long enough, we become at home in the neighbourhood. Reminiscences spring up, like flowers, about uninteresting corners. We forget to some degree the superior loveliness of other places, and fall into a tolerant and sympathetic spirit which is its own reward and justification. Looking back the other day on some recollections of my own, I was astonished to find how much I owed to such a residence; six weeks in one unpleasant country-side had done more, it seemed, to quicken and educate my sensibilities than many years in places that jumped more nearly with my inclination.

The country to which I refer was a level and treeless plateau, over which the winds cut like a whip. For miles on miles it was the same. A river, indeed, fell into the sea near the town where I resided; but the valley of the river was shallow and bald for as far up as ever I had the heart to follow it. There were roads, certainly, but roads that had no beauty or interest; for, as there was no timber, and but little irregularity of surface, you saw your whole walk exposed to you from the beginning: there was nothing left to fancy, nothing to expect, nothing to see by the wayside, save here and there an unhomely-looking homestead, and here and there a solitary, spectacled stone-breaker; and you were only accompanied, as you went doggedly forward, by the gaunt telegraph-posts and the hum of the resonant wires in the keen sea-wind. To one who had learned to know their song in warm pleasant places by the Mediterranean, it seemed to taunt the country, and make it still bleaker by suggested contrast. Even the waste places by the side of the road were not, as Hawthorne[10] liked to put it, "taken back to Nature" by any decent covering of vegetation. Wherever the land had the chance, it seemed to lie fallow. There is a certain tawny nudity of the South, bare sunburnt plains, coloured like a lion, and hills clothed only in the blue transparent air; but this was of another description—this was the nakedness of the North; the earth seemed to know that it was naked, and was ashamed and cold.

It seemed to be always blowing on that coast. Indeed, this had passed into the speech of the inhabitants, and they saluted each other when they met with "Breezy, breezy," instead of the customary "Fine day" of farther south. These continual winds were not like the harvest breeze, that just keeps an equable pressure against your face as you walk, and serves to set all the trees talking over your head, or bring round you the smell of the wet surface of the country after a shower. They were of the bitter, hard, persistent sort, that interferes with sight and respiration, and makes the eyes sore. Even such winds as these have their own merit in proper time and place. It is pleasant to see them brandish great masses of shadow. And what a power they have over the colour of the world! How they ruffle the solid woodlands in their passage, and make them shudder and whiten like a single willow! There is nothing more vertiginous than a wind like this among the woods, with all its sights and noises; and the effect gets between some painters and their sober eyesight, so that, even when the rest of their picture is calm, the foliage is coloured like foliage in a gale. There was nothing, however, of this sort to be noticed in a country where there were no trees and hardly any shadows, save the passive shadows of clouds or those of rigid houses and walls. But the wind was nevertheless an occasion of pleasure; for nowhere could you taste more fully the pleasure of a sudden lull, or a place of opportune shelter. The reader knows what I mean;

10. Nathaniel Hawthorne (1804–1864), American novelist and short story writer.

he must remember how, when he has sat himself down behind a dyke on a hill-side, he delighted to hear the wind hiss vainly through the crannies at his back; how his body tingled all over with warmth, and it began to dawn upon him, with a sort of slow surprise, that the country was beautiful, the heather purple, and the faraway hills all marbled with sun and shadow. Wordsworth, in a beautiful passage of the "Prelude,"[11] has used this as a figure for the feeling struck in us by the quiet by-streets of London after the uproar of the great thoroughfares; and the comparison may be turned the other way with as good effect:

> "Meanwhile the roar continues, till at length,
> Escaped as from an enemy, we turn
> Abruptly into some sequester'd nook,
> Still as a shelter'd place when winds blow loud!"[12]

I remember meeting a man once, in a train, who told me of what must have been quite the most perfect instance of this pleasure of escape. He had gone up, one sunny, windy morning, to the top of a great cathedral somewhere abroad; I think it was Cologne Cathedral, the great unfinished marvel by the Rhine;[13] and after a long while in dark stairways, he issued at last into the sunshine, on a platform high above the town. At that elevation it was quite still and warm; the gale was only in the lower strata of the air, and he had forgotten it in the quiet interior of the church and during his long ascent; and so you may judge of his surprise when, resting his arms on the sunlit balustrade and looking over into the *Place*[14] far below him, he saw the good people holding on

11. Wordsworth wrote three versions of *The Prelude, or Growth of a Poet's Mind*: the first in 1799, an expanded version in 1805–6, and a revised version in 1850.
12. From Book VII, "Residence in London," 168–71 (1850).
13. Construction on Cologne Cathedral, one of the largest Gothic structures in the world, began in 1248. The project was completed in 1880, six years after the publication of Stevenson's essay.
14. The Square.

their hats and leaning hard against the wind as they walked. There is something, to my fancy, quite perfect in this little experience of my fellow-traveller's. The ways of men seem always very trivial to us when we find ourselves alone on a church top, with the blue sky and a few tall pinnacles, and see far below us the steep roofs and foreshortened buttresses, and the silent activity of the city streets; but how much more must they not have seemed so to him as he stood, not only above other men's business, but above other men's climate, in a golden zone like Apollo's.

This was the sort of pleasure I found in the country of which I write. The pleasure was to be out of the wind, and to keep it in memory all the time, and hug oneself upon the shelter. And it was only by the sea that any such sheltered places were to be found. Between the black worm-eaten headlands there are little bights and havens, well screened from the wind and the commotion of the external sea, where the sand and weeds look up into the gazer's face from a depth of tranquil water, and the sea-birds, screaming and flickering from the ruined crags, alone disturb the silence and the sunshine. One such place has impressed itself on my memory beyond all others. On a rock by the water's edge, old fighting men of the Norse breed had planted a double castle; the two stood wall to wall like semi-detached villas; and yet feud had run so high between their owners, that one, from out of a window, shot the other as he stood in his own doorway. There is something in the juxtaposition of these two enemies full of tragic irony. It is grim to think of bearded men and bitter women taking hateful counsel together about the two hall-fires at night, when the sea boomed against the foundations and the wild winter wind was loose over the battlements. And in the study we may reconstruct for ourselves some pale figure of what life then was. Not so when we are there; when we are there such thoughts come to us only to intensify a contrary impression, and association is turned against itself. I remember walking thither three afternoons in succession, my eyes weary with being set against the wind, and how, dropping suddenly over the edge of the down, I found myself in a new world of warmth and shelter. The wind, from which I had escaped, "as from an enemy," was seemingly quite local. It carried no clouds with it, and came from such a quarter that it did not trouble the sea within view. The two castles, black and ruinous as the rocks about them, were still distinguishable from these by something more insecure and fantastic in the outline, something that the last storm had left imminent and the next would demolish entirely. It would be difficult to render in words the sense of peace that took possession of me on these three afternoons. It was helped out, as I have said, by the contrast. The shore was battered and bemauled by previous tempests; I had the memory at heart of the insane strife of the pigmies who had erected these two castles and lived in them in mutual distrust and enmity, and knew I had only to put my head out of this little cup of shelter to find the hard wind blowing in my eyes; and yet there were the two great tracts of motionless blue air and peaceful sea looking on, unconcerned and apart, at the turmoil of the present moment and the memorials of the precarious past. There is ever something transitory and fretful in the impression of a high wind under a cloudless sky; it seems to have no root in the constitution of things; it must speedily begin to faint and wither away like a cut flower. And on those days the thought of the wind and the thought of human life came very near together in my mind. Our noisy years did indeed seem moments in the being of the eternal silence:[15] and the wind, in the face of that great field of stationary blue, was as the wind of a

15. From Wordsworth's "Intimations of Immortality from Recollections of Early Childhood" (1807):

> Those shadowy recollections,
> Which, be they what they may,
> Are yet the fountain-light of all our day,
> Are yet a master-light of all our seeing;
> Uphold us, cherish, and have power to make
> Our noisy years seem moments in the being
> Of the eternal Silence (153–60)

butterfly's wing. The placidity of the sea was a thing likewise to be remembered. Shelley speaks of the sea as "hungering for calm,"[16] and in this place one learned to understand the phrase. Looking down into these green waters from the broken edge of the rock, or swimming leisurely in the sunshine, it seemed to me that they were enjoying their own tranquillity; and when now and again it was disturbed by a wind ripple on the surface, or the quick black passage of a fish far below, they settled back again (one could fancy) with relief.

On shore too, in the little nook of shelter, everything was so subdued and still that the least particular struck in me a pleasurable surprise. The desultory crackling of the whin-pods[17] in the afternoon sun usurped the ear. The hot, sweet breath of the bank, that had been saturated all day long with sunshine, and now exhaled it into my face, was like the breath of a fellow-creature. I remember that I was haunted by two lines of French verse; in some dumb way they seemed to fit my surroundings and give expression to the contentment that was in me, and I kept repeating to myself—

> "Mon cœur est un luth suspendu,
> Sitôt qu'on le touche, il résonne."[18]

I can give no reason why these lines came to me at this time; and for that very cause I repeat them here. For all I know, they may

---

16. From *Prometheus Unbound* (1820):

> Their white arms lifted o'er their streaming hair
> With garlands pied and starry sea-flower crowns,
> Hastening to grace their mighty sister's joy.
> It is the unpastured sea hungering for calm. (3.2.45–49)

17. The seedpods of spiny gorse.
18. "My heart is a lute newly strung, / Just one touch, and it resounds." From "Le Refus" ("The Refusal") by French poet and songwriter Pierre-Jean de Béranger (1780–1857).

serve to complete the impression in the mind of the reader, as they were certainly a part of it for me.

And this happened to me in the place of all others where I liked least to stay. When I think of it I grow ashamed of my own ingratitude. "Out of the strong came forth sweetness."[19] There, in the bleak and gusty North, I received, perhaps, my strongest impression of peace. I saw the sea to be great and calm; and the earth, in that little corner, was all alive and friendly to me. So, wherever a man is, he will find something to please and pacify him: in the town he will meet pleasant faces of men and women, and see beautiful flowers at a window, or hear a cage-bird singing at the corner of the gloomiest street; and for the country, there is no country without some amenity—let him only look for it in the right spirit, and he will surely find.

19. Stevenson is alluding to Samson's honey riddle. When a beehive is discovered in the rotting carcass of a lion, Samson proclaims: "Out of the eater came forth meat, and out of the strong came forth sweetness" (Judges 14:14) Out of unpleasantness comes forth joy.

www.ingramcontent.com/pod-product-compliance
Lightning Source LLC
Chambersburg PA
CBHW070630310726
48982CB00001B/228
* 9 7 8 1 5 1 6 5 5 7 1 8 9 *